MIGHTY MERRY TOO
AND THE GRANDMOTHER WHO WENT TO SEA

MARY MCCOLLUM

MERRY PUBLISHING
LA CROSSE, WISCONSIN

D0862359

Published by Merry Publishing

Registered with the IP Rights Office
Copyright Registration Service
Ref: 219781843

Thank you to Mike_Lakin at Davenport_maps for permission to use excerpts from Davenport maps.

Thank you to the University of Texas for making so many maps available to the Public Domain

ISBN-10   0-9793797-0-9
ISBN-13   978-0-9793797-0-3

PROLOGUE
MY MOTHER RAN OFF TO SEA

Yes, my mother did run off to sea. Just before her 55th birthday she announced, "I'm going to retire, sell my house and everything in it to go sailing all the time." This announcement came shortly after her return from a two-month summer vacation spent sailing the Great Lakes. Was I surprised? Well, yes and no. She'd always been just a little unconventional, more often out of necessity than choice. As she put it, "necessity often taught the value of being different", but as time passed her unconventional behavior was more often by choice. When she was rescued after being injured between Fiji and New Zealand, Michael, my 12-year-old son said, "I think it's time Grandma sold that boat and bought a house." She didn't.

Her mother, my grandmother, warned, "Don't you ever give your mother a hard time for doing what she wants at this stage of life. Even if she doesn't live as long because of it she shouldn't grow old thinking of the things she wished she had done." Grandma was 90 when she made that statement, so we figured she knew what she was talking about.

Probably what troubled me, as well as my brother and sister, a bit was the fact that our mother was doing this alone. Still, she had done so much alone. I was only six when dad stepped out of our life. Later, she remarried, and as she put it, "she married a sailboat". While the duration of the marriage was short, it seemed to be a turning point in her life. So, as long as her mind was made up, we decided to enjoy her long and enthusiastic letters describing her adventures as well as her occasional fly-in visits. After all, she was here for the birth of each of our children so she could play the grandmother role.

I suppose I occasionally felt a little cheated while striding down the halls of Mass General Hospital, feeling pretty good over a particularly difficult achievement, when one of my colleagues rushed up and asked, "Where's your mother now?" I can't tell her story however so I'm turning this over to her; Mary of the *MIGHTY MERRY TOO.*

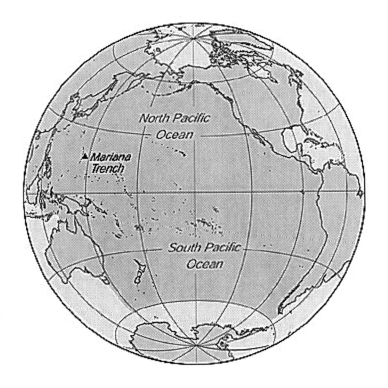

MIGHTY MERRY TOO'S HOME OCEAN

MIGHTY MERRY TOO'S EXPLORATORY ROUTE

CHAPTER ONE
CHANGING MY LIFE

This is a chronicle of adventures and misadventures, which are best, understood in the framework of my background. I am small, and my hair turned gray while I was still very young, so today it does seem natural to describe myself as a little gray haired grandmother. I'm telling it because so many who are aware of the bits and pieces have pleaded with me to tell the whole story as well as answer the many questions I'm repeatedly asked. Where did my sense of independence come? How did I learn to deal with fear? How did I learn to accept the weeks of solitude a long passage imposes? Additionally, once I start my tale so many wonderful memories come flooding back until the writing of it becomes a joyful effort but answering those questions does require a lot of history.

My dad was the picture of Americana: he had been raised in an immigrant family. We worked hard to find some of their early history. His father died while I was very young so my memory is of what I heard. Dad never talked about that early history but we've found a lot of records including his arrival at Ellis Island on the Pretoria.

First Name: Wladislaw
Last Name: Milewsky
Ethnicity: Russia, Lithuanian
Last Place of Residence: Kupiski, Russia
Date of Arrival: May 09, 1905
Age at Arrival: 40y   Gender: M   Marital Status: M
Ship of Travel: Pretoria
Port of Departure: Hamburg   Manifest Line Number: 0014

THE PRETORIA

Dad was born back in what was then Russia and today is Lithuania If the records are correct would have been old enough to have remembered some of the trip but I never heard him speak of it.

He had attended a Polish Catholic grade school in Grand Rapids, Michigan, a school where he was taught in Polish. It was the same parish where his father was organist. He served in the army during WW I after dropping out of high school perhaps because he didn't know enough English to be successful. He then went in to the army where he taught balloon flight so he must have improved his English pretty fast. We found his military papers during a genealogical search. I never heard a trace of anything but Midwestern English in his speech. He subsequently enrolled in a technological school where he earned a pharmacy license, which was just a matter of weeks in those days. He followed that with several other courses which led him eventually to setting up a commercial photography business: that business failed along with so much else in 1929.

While I heard about these events from my mother; what I heard from my dad was, "Anybody can do anything once they set their mind to it." It wasn't a once only statement. He was a demonstration of that attitude. After losing the photography business he soon found employment as advertising manager for a local business which manufactured machines for making concrete blocks. In the milieu of that business environment he came across a new machine he believed was more productive than his employer was producing. The patent was for sale. After a futile attempt to convince that employer to buy the patent he bought the patent himself and set up a competitive manufacturing business in the same small town of Holland, Michigan. In such a small town where it seemed everyone knew everyone else the odds were against him. National and even international sales were no problem but employing the locals for the manufacturing process was. His answer to that was to farm the production out around the state until it happened that an ideal local building became available at an ideal price. Once he started producing locally he simply paid the highest wages in town and still made a profit. Unions were very active and he was determined not to have to fight them as well as the fact he believed it to be a productive practice; well paid employees would be productive. Like his daughter later he did all that on borrowed money which was completely repaid by the time of his premature death.

Mother's history was quite different but led to similar resourcefulness and independence. She came from a rural farming family in a community outside Grand Rapids; they had a long history in the US and

Canada. I often chuckled as she proudly talked about the fact that she had her own horse and buggy to get to high school in the nearby small town. After graduation she left the farm for her own apartment in the big city of Grand Rapids where she quickly became employed in a large department store. This was at a time when not many women were so independent. I found her saved letters after her death including those from the many service men she wrote to during the war. They included Dad. Those letters gave a picture of their youth which I find precious.

I spent a bit of time with dad and he stated his belief in the human potential many times under many conditions. My parents were very caring and within the range of depression economics were probably also quite indulgent but times were very different back then. I was probably nine or ten years old when I learned to swim, long before we lived down by the lake. I rode my bike to a friend's house where many of my classmates were swimming. One side of the dock was shallow and one side deep. I stayed on the shallow side because I couldn't swim but suddenly a group of them came over, picked me up and threw me in to the deep side. I learned to swim. Today swimming lessons would seem more appropriate.

I attended a small rural school; four rooms for eight grades. Actually three room since kindergarten had a room to itself. One had to learn to apply oneself and be quiet while a different grade was receiving the teacher's attention. There was a lot of benefit to that but in some ways it lead to my laziness. Since I was a pretty noisy talky child the teacher for sixth, seventh, and eighth grade, simply gave me extra work to do to keep me quiet. The result was that when I entered the "city" high school I had already com-pleted the course work for all my classes. Was it a real surprise that in nice weather I was off on my bicycle instead of in class? Finally the assistant principal called me in "to cut a deal." My absences would be ignored if I would quite convincing other people to go with me. Maybe my teachers simply appreciated my absences. My "talkiness" served me well in Spanish class where my teacher announced she didn't care how much I talked to others in the class as long as it was in Spanish. No English.

My sailing history goes way back to World War II years. Individuality and responsibility were both encouraged and expected. I became almost like an only child after December 7, 1941, when my two older brothers went off to war. Once more my mother showed her independence. Don, the younger of my two brothers, had enlisted but developed a severe strep infection before being inducted. The family doctor sent a telegram to the proper authorities which communicated Don's delay. Antibiotics were new and scarce since they went to the military and the same physician warned any movement of him would be life threatening. The response from the military authorities was that they would be sending an ambulance for him. Mother sat on the front porch with her hunting shot gun on her lap waiting for them to arrive. Given the doctor's advice she wasn't going to let them take her son. The ambulance never arrived and Don recovered and was then inducted.

I was a bit more indulged but those indulgences certainly still carried the expectation of responsibility. Such responsibility was very well defined; I, like anybody, could do anything if willing to work hard enough for it but nobody else could do it for me.

In our neighborhood there were lots of boys my age, most of them owners of small racing sailboats, but I was the only girl. The local yacht club sponsored races whenever there were five or more of the same class: a class being boats of the same size and design. I had numerous opportunities to day sail on a small cruising sailboat owned by acquaintances, which gave me the opportunity to watch the boys race while being a helper on the bigger boat. I didn't know enough to call myself crew. These opportunities to watch simply whet my appetite. While I didn't dare nag, or even hope for that matter, I certainly dropped lots and lots of hints about how wonderful it would be if I had a boat.

One of dad's recreations was at the card table. He played at a private men's club, and I heard about his consistent winnings from several of my high school friends who worked there as bus boys after school. One day he came home with a trailer behind the car. We always assumed he had won the sailboat that was on that trailer in a card game. His only comment was," You can have it if you can figure out how to get it in the water." She was a snipe; a 15 ½ foot one design racing dinghy; a very popular design world wide still today. I emphasize again that I knew his attitude; anyone can do anything if they really want to so I certainly believed I could get it in the water.

Remember, this was the mid forties so we are talking about a wood boat and all the effort it takes to prepare a wood boat for a summer of sailing: scraping off the old paint, caulking the seams, and finally painting enough coats to keep the wood protected. At least it was fresh water. It was much later when I learned what salt water can do to a paint job. The boat arrived in the spring with plenty of time remaining before the sailing season, which is pretty short in Michigan. Did my friends help me? Of course not, they were too busy with their own boats. Dad was generous however. I was able to go to the local marine yard and buy any tool I needed for the job: hand tools that is. I never saw an electric sander or a paint sprayer but I did see lots and lots of sand paper and caulking material. Looking back I think the men at the boat yard were very helpful by advising me what tools to buy as well as how to use them. For a very young novice however I really did do a reasonable job.

Then one day it was time to launch her. I doubt that dad realized just how little I really knew, but I was perfectly confident that I could learn by doing. She was a centerboard boat, so if she should capsize she would simply turn over and float upside down: I could swim. The biggest problem with a capsize, in my mind, was the hazard to the sails. Those were the days of canvas sails. I had visited the sail maker who gave me a long lecture on the care of my sails which included the warning about them being stretched out of shape if left taut when wet. In other words if one capsized, halyards (the lines hauling them taut) needed to be released. After launching I actually did manage to sail her, day after day after day.

By now the war was over and my oldest brother, Walt, was home. At his request I took him out one day; the only day I ever capsized her. I suppose one of the reasons I remember it so distinctly is due to Walt's reaction. It actually was quite easy to crawl out of the water up onto the upside down hull which he promptly did. There he was up in the sunshine, all the while complaining about how cold he was while I was diving underneath trying to release the halyards as well as begging him to help. He has never accompanied me since. To top it off I was towed home by neighbors who never let me forget my need for their assistance; until, finally, the next spring their dog managed to get into an enclosed porch at our house to steal our Easter Ham. Embarrassment meeting embarrassment equals silence.

True enough, I certainly did learn a lot by doing: fortunately after a few weeks we heard the Yacht Club was offering a sailing class for which I promptly signed up. I quickly learned there was a whole lot I didn't know; probably I absorbed that much more of what was taught because of the experience I now had. All summer long the Yacht Club held sailboat races every Saturday afternoon for any class of boat with 5 or more entrants. Eventually we got five Snipe owners together and one Saturday afternoon we had an official race. I faced a problem preparing for it; while sailing the little craft by myself was very easy I was required to have a crew for a race. Where to find that crew? Many of the local young people had their own boat and those that didn't were mostly taken up as crew on somebody else's boat. Those that weren't were males. This was the early forties remember, and what teen age boy would crew for a girl? Not many believe me, but there was one, and I remember him with great fondness. We came in first place. Never again were we able to get five together to have another race. I wonder why? From my Snipe I graduated a few years later to a Star, an Olympic class boat at the time, but there were never enough Stars on our lake to have an official race, so up to this day I can say I won every race I ever entered.

WINK, MY STAR

Then came college followed by marriage to a man I met at the same university. He was in graduate school at the time. Family responsibilities followed as well as a very sad interval; dad was drowned at the time of the birth of my first child. The last time I spent with him was as he was walking me down the aisle at my wedding.

We had more children, despite family planning and life became more difficult. John 1, my husband, changed from law school to medical school, from the State of Utah to the State of Michigan. It was becoming obvious John had emotional problems but giving up just wasn't something I knew about.

That marriage ended when, after the birth of our three children and three short days after my delivery of a still born child, my husband, in collaboration with his mother, presented me with the knowledge he not only wanted a divorce but also wanted to relieve himself of all responsibility. To say that his method of presenting it was dramatic is a vast understatement.

My first day out of the hospital, a Saturday, he and his mother took me to see the grave of the stillborn and from there to the office building of a very prominent group of lawyers with no explanation. Being Saturday the building was almost empty and mostly dark. I was ushered in to a large conference table. While they exited a lawyer presented himself, asking if I understood why I was there. No, in fact I didn't understand but I was promptly informed. My husband wanted a divorce. Since I had no visible means of support I obviously couldn't care for the three children, 2, 4, and 6 years of age. He didn't want the responsibility for them so they would be adopted individually by an aunt and two cousins. Since his grandfather was head of the children's welfare agency there would be no problem arranging for that. The lawyer was not going to ask me to sign any papers today but did give them to me to peruse and we departed. I was speechless. In fact one might say this was my first time at sea, long before my voyages across the Pacific.

We got back in the car and I made sure I was on the outside edge of the three seater front seat rather than trapped between the two. Not having the slightest idea what I was going to do and realizing I had only coins in my purse as well as the fact that I was in Salt Lake City, far away from my home territory I simply got out of the car at a stop light and started walking. What was I going to do?

After walking a short distance I saw a taxi and even knowing I didn't have the money to pay for it I hailed the driver. Once in the cab I remembered the one friendly and influential person I knew in this town. With no reason to believe he would be in his office on a Saturday I gave that location to the driver and then puzzled, what was I expecting? There was one car there. Telling the driver that I would be back to pay him in a moment I went inside, down the corridor to an open door, walked in and found Otto, a friend of my father's sitting at his desk. He was more than startled to see me. I quickly blurted out the fact I needed his help, the first step being to pay the cab waiting outside. I didn't realize until he told me just how fortunate I was to find him there. He had moved his principal office to another state and had just flown in for a very few hours to go over some issues at this plant.

While I very much wanted to cry I believed I simply had to keep control. After all I had three children to think of. I will quickly come to the end of a long harrowing tale. Otto loaned me some cash(I had no credit card in those days) and found a lawyer for me. After persuading him to come to his office on Saturday Otto took me to the lawyer's office. The lawyer, Tom, provided encouragement but it was obvious it was not going to be an easy road. His first admonition was that I must call my mother.

That phone call was probably the most difficult phone call I have ever made. I was the one who had chosen this marriage and all that went with it. In my mind I had no right to go back home to mother, especially since she had been struggling ever since dad's death. But, as Tom pointed out, it was a destination where I had contacts; I knew people and was known. He obtained a court order for child support, most of which was not received. I was always convinced that John's mother provided what little did arrive. He simply disappeared.

Tom was right regarding the decision to return to my home town and state, thousands of miles away. We ended up on the San Francisco Flyer taking us as far as Chicago. Don, my youngest child became slightly feverish and broken out all over in a severe rash. He was so sick in fact that the train stopped at a service point in Wyoming and a doctor was brought on board. He diagnosed Don as having measles; he should be kept quiet, in a darkened space and away from other people. Ouch. I had to change trains in Chicago; not just trains but train stations. I was fearful that if noticed, the health authorities would want to quarantine him. Well, it all happened.

By the time we got back to Holland, Michigan I had a plan. I can't imagine that what I did could be accomplished today but I went to our local bank. I explained how poor I was, that I had decided I needed a teaching certificate because if I needed to support these children, the time frame of a teacher's life is more suitable for the circumstances. Therefore, I needed to borrow enough money to live on for a year to be paid back on an annual basis over 10 years. Yes, they loaned it to me and off I went to Michigan State University, three small children in tow.

With family responsibilities there was never time or money for the luxuries of sailing but sailing was a joy I never forgot and somehow I always knew that I would enjoy a long distance passage every bit as much as I loved all the day sailing I did.

As my children matured and moved off on their own, I became involved in another romance and even a brief marriage. When asked about that marriage I usually say, "I married a sailboat." When Dick and I became involved it usually was with outdoor activities; we hiked, camped and he taught me to ride a motorcycle. We bought a pair of motorcycles; two Hondas; mine a 250/4, small for a short lady, his a 500/4.

He spent many hours teaching me motorcycle safety while we practiced on Sundays on the driver ed lots of local schools. By the time I took my driver's test I passed with flying colors and, as a matter of fact, I found a lot of pleasure riding that bike. I rode it to work on occasion. In nice weather I frequently rode it to work wearing a pair of coveralls over proper business clothes. When attending an academic meeting of one sort or another I stuffed the coveralls under the seat and walked in carrying my motorcycle helmet. One special memory is the day when I was on an express way leaving the city of Detroit. Two motorcycle police came along and escorted me, one in front and one in back, through the traffic. They didn't depart until a suburban motorcycle policeman took over the escort. It was before the days when women had found equality but they were often given consideration.

Dick frequently had blocks of free time that allowed for pretty big projects and had access to a boat mooring in front of a friend's house. We came across a wooden racing boat for sale; one of only seven boats that had been designed and built for a private club. She was 29 feet long, keel, with a sleek and attractive design. While the severe winters of Michigan required hauling a small boat out of the water in the winter, being out of the water for a long time is very hard on it. This was the case for our great find. We began to work together on the boat and by the time she was ready to go into the water we felt very close and we married. We had many hours of pleasure sailing her. Eventually however he became uncomfortable about my capacity on the tiller which I began to realize was really a part of a bigger problem; the local economy.

All of this was during a time when the Midwest was earning the title of "Rust Belt" and it all affected Dick's business as well. He had a tendency toward depression and when that depression started leading him to irrational behavior I determined I had to leave him. Irrational behavior? Changing his business phone number to an unlisted number for example. Worse was violence toward me. It was a simple almost do it yourself divorce but it was a painful time for me. Here I was the eternal optimist married to a man fighting depression and I could not make my optimism contagious. Additionally I had twice made a bad choice.

Although we were together only a little more than two years it was a time of learning for me: more than motorcycle riding. I began to understand who I was and what I could and couldn't do. Despite my dad's teachings that I could do anything I set my mind to do I realized I couldn't take responsibility for someone else's emotions. Nor could I necessarily change them. Dick cared about me but he was very unhappy with himself. We met several time over the next few years and we had long conversations but recognized we needed to each go our own way.

That renewal of my sailing experience finally led me, as a middle aged single adult, to owning my own boat. Fiberglass!!!! There was still the bottom to scrape and paint and trim to varnish but no more caulking. Yes, I was still doing my own prep. She was a pretty little Cape Dory Typhoon often still described as "America's littlest Yacht."

My eldest son, Michael and his wife bought it from me when they moved to Florida which gave me the excuse to buy a bit larger boat by the same designer and sailing characteristics. I promptly christened her "Mighty Merry", which I thought was a very clever pun, but I was always amazed at the number of people who wouldn't differentiate between Mary and Merry. They made it clear they thought me quite arrogant.

This boat contained a galley, head and sleeping accommodations which quickly set me to thinking about cruising the Great Lakes so I began to collect charts, learn a bit more about navigation. I also manipulated my work at Oakland Community College so I could take two months unpaid vacation every summer. I paid the penalty when I returned because nobody took over my responsibilities in the financial aid office while I was gone but I made it work never the less.

By this time I had a berth at the Detroit Yacht Club, having become only the 2nd woman to have a membership in her own name. There were a number of women belonging to the club who were widows of members and of course many spouses of members that participated in boating but only my friend Peg and I were voting members and Peg did not yet own a boat. On the day the board of directors was elected only voting members were allowed in the club. Dinner and drinks were free to encourage a good turnout for voting. When we had difficulties getting in past the gate on voting night perhaps I should have just chuckled; to the guards it was just automatic for women not to be allowed through on election night, but I did find it more than irritating.

Through the following years I sponsored a number of members, a goodly number of whom were women. Most of them did not own boats but participated in a sailing instruction class provided every spring and quickly became active in the fleet of single class racing boats owned by the Club. My neighbor on the dock was a power boat. The owner was forever telling me how to do this and that. On the last election night that I remember being there he had run for an office which he won, and in celebration followed it up with a heavy indulgence in the free drinks. When he spotted me he came over and drew a big crowd around him to tell them how expertly I handled Mighty Merry. This attitude was quite a revelation to me.

The Great Lakes provide some delightful fresh water cruising with each of the lakes offering very different environments. The first summer with Mighty Merry the furthest I roamed was down the Detroit River to Lake Erie and across to Ohio. The next summer I arranged for a full two months away from the office and I became a bit more venturesome, heading north to Canadian waters where I discovered the Sweet Water Sea of Georgian Bay and the 30 thousand islands. As I thumb through photos I took up there and the memories come flooding back I realize I still have an enormous fondness for those waters; waters still clean enough to drink directly from the bay. They weren't warm for swimming like the tropical waters, but they were a welcoming environment; far enough away from city and suburban life to feel adventuresome, as well as being alone enough of the time to feel both the peace and violence that Mother Nature provides.

MIGHTY MERRY IN ONTARIO

One summer as I was preparing for the summer's cruise I broke my hand. I was numb with the realization that I couldn't sail Mighty

Merry one handed. Single handed or solo, yes, but one handed no. I was dragging my feet as I came home that afternoon. Diane, the young college student who cleaned my home for me was still there finishing up the task. I knew Diane was an outdoor person, an athlete, as well as being ambitious, bright and a talented art student. "Diane, what are you doing this summer?" I hadn't thought out what I was about to ask but when her answer was, "just go to summer school," I impulsively asked, "how would you like to spend the summer sailing with me?" That broken hand provided the basis for a developing friendship that has endured 'til even her parents call me her adopted mother. She did spend the summer with me, and we did travel up to Lake Huron and down Lake Michigan to the waters and harbors where I had grown up. I felt such a sense of achievement when I sailed through the channel into Lake Macatawa and visited the family with whom I had first sailed as a very young girl.

I had my first experience with Mother Nature's violence during that trip; a thunderstorm as we sailed down the coast of Lake Michigan. That storm behaved quite differently than most I've known in that it came to us from the West as most do, passed over and then reversed and came back over us again. I truly was a bit frightened but didn't dare show my fright because I felt I needed to demonstrate confidence to Diane. I wonder if I ever told her that?

I didn't bring Mighty Merry back to the Yacht Club any more. Instead I left her where I was at the end of my sailing vacation because I no longer had any interest in the day sails on the Detroit River or Lake St. Claire and my interest in the Yacht club wasn't the elaborate parties. One September I hauled her and left her in a marina located almost at the top of Michigan's Lower Peninsula. A young man offered to paint her hull so she would look like new and never again need wax. Anything that would reduce the prep work sounded wonderful to me. Until recently he had worked in a Detroit area car plant where they made fiberglass sports cars. There he had been taught the skills needed to work with some of the modern specialized paints. The price was right and the job was done right, although I suspect he learned a lot about estimating since it took him much longer than he expected. The contract had been a set price rather than an hourly rate. She was gorgeous, on the outside at least.

I began to think about upgrading her interior. While up on one of the many islands of Georgian Bay (the pseudonym for this area being the 30 Thousand Islands) I met a Canadian craftsman and his wife, first generation German immigrants, who were sailing an example of his craftsmanship. The Ontario economy was in hard shape at the time so his well equipped workshop in back of his house was drawing very little business. We favored some of the same anchorages so we met on a number of occasions. His wife invariably invited me for a rich and sinful dessert which she had made on board. While my galley was a bit like camping, once at anchor she had the luxuries of a gourmet kitchen. He had a Honda generator with an enormously long power cord led to his battery system. He knew that anyone who made the effort to get into these remote waters would be violently averse to listening to the noise of a generator so he took it far across the many enormous boulders to be found on shore. She had all the electricity she wanted and we had quiet.

We sketched out some ideas of improving my galley and cabin usage. Once I found what I liked he offered a flat price to do the job in his shop over the winter. I would have the boat hauled at a Parry Sound marina; he would trailer it to his workshop and have it ready for me in the spring in time to relaunch in the same marina. I tried to hide my gasp when I saw the price he offered; literally half of what I expected. Of course I agreed and come the following spring I was as pleased with his work as I had been with the price.

That fall I came home and settled back in to the office; my whole world changed within days. That first day back I learned about a condo, walking distance from my office which was for sale at a rock bottom price. It was on a ravine quite deep in a wooded area with a feeling of great privacy, considering it was a condo, and I had coveted that location for some time. The woman was in great haste as she was marrying and leaving the state so she grabbed my extremely low offer.

When I had completed the paper work on that purchase I was still working my way down through the pile of mail on my office desk that had waited for me over the summer and I read a document from the president's office. What? The college was offering anyone 55 and over the opportunity to retire with a pension calculated as though they had worked until 65 if that person would agree to not accept employment in any public educational institution in Michigan. A decision needed to be made by x date. I gasped. I was to turn 55 within a few days. I had started a career late, after John 1 walked out and disappeared. Thus, my expectation was that I would have to work much past the usual 65 in order to have a reasonable retirement. The offer included a consultation with a specialist in estate planning etc. so I certainly took them up on that part of the offer. Let's see whether I could afford this venture. No, he advised, I certainly could not.

Well, now, just what does he know about what I can do? He's basing his advice on the average suburbanite but I don't want to be an average suburbanite. What do I want to do? First of all I want the freedom to decide what I want to do: this offer certainly provides that. My children are all off on their own now: they didn't all accept the help they were offered during late adolescence but they are now all independent and none of them expecting or asking for help from me. Probably what I want to do is just go sailing.

Hmmmm. Well, you are having your little cruising boat upgraded right at this very moment. If you sell everything else, move onto the boat your cost of living will go way down. Along with this pension comes a guarantee of health and dental insurance as well. But Mary, you have two mortgages on two residences so you have to sell those. Yes, but there will be the rest of this academic year with a salary and you need a place to live during those months anyway: that means you have nine months to figure solutions to the rest of the problem. You can figure almost anything out in nine months. If I can't get them sold I'll set up a consulting service to the many private colleges in the area until the economy improves and I can sell them. I've built up enough of a reputation in my field that will work. So my thoughts went until I signed the contract to accept the early retirement as of June 26 the following spring of 1986.

Very few of my colleagues took up the option on the basis that they "just didn't know what to do with their time" if they were to do that. This was despite the fact a few of them acknowledged it just didn't pay them to go to work, i.e. they would take home more money retired than employed. If someone offered you the freedom to every day choose what you would do with your time and every month on the 23rd day money would appear in your bank account what would you do? Don't you imagine that you would think up some pretty interesting things to do? Well, I knew I could.

How much money would appear every month? Yes, there was the question whether the magic money was sufficient. It was magic money because it felt like money I hadn't earned, which in my lexicon is "magic money." Sufficient as defined by an amount to provide for the longer future of a 55-year-old in contrast to a 65-year-old: a longer future in addition to the indulgence of world travel. Actually it was a pretty big question for me because not only had I started a career a bit later than many, additionally I had obtained the education allowing me to enter that career on borrowed money after becoming the sole support of three small children. Unlike many women a generation later, I often worked at a somewhat lower pay scale. Thus, of course, the basis for the resulting pension would be lower.

Today it is embarrassing to look back and realize the degree to which I didn't know how much I needed to have. When I had been a young single parent terrified of the responsibilities I faced I had always lived way beyond my means; my education was financed by borrowed money, viewed as an investment. We lived in a neighborhood with good schools despite the higher cost of living incurred. When those responsibilities were in the past, I was so in the habit of overspending it just felt like being a good American to always maintain a good wardrobe, membership in a good tennis club, and a car without a hint of rust or heavy oil consumption. All of that left little for saving but by then I had gained the confidence to believe I would always earn more and more money from year to year and eventually live within my means.

I did know however, that during my adolescence I had experienced moderate affluence at home but still succeeded in adjusting to frugality when near poverty raised its ugly head in my mid twenties. Hadn't I proven my adaptability? When the financial consultant advised that I simply couldn't afford to retire and should plan to work a number of additional years despite this attractive offer I thought to myself, "how does he know what I can accomplish?" After all, I had talked to a financial consultant once before, in the very early years of responsibility, he had shook his head and said, "You just can't afford to survive." He was a friend and neighbor with whom I have lost touch but I sometimes wish he could see me today. In consequence, despite not having a grasp of my financial needs, despite my training and experience as an accountant, I grabbed what I saw as the chance for total freedom; a true rarity for anyone in modern society. I would finish the academic year and then be free.

That fall was exceptionally warm and sunny in Michigan. One October weekend I was sitting under the oak tree in front, sanding some of the bright work I had brought home from my little sailing vessel when a young man walked by, stared at me for a moment and blurted out, "Where's Nancy?" After learning that I had purchased Nancy's residence and she had married and moved to Florida he blurted out again, "But I wanted to buy it." So buy it he did but from me rather than Nancy and with a 20% profit for having lived in it for a few days, with nary a real estate agent or lawyer involved and I had solved one of the many problems facing me. Daring you say? What if something went sour and it had to later go through the courts? Would I be sorry for not having a lawyer write up the paper work properly? No, because that is just what did happen years later and my "homemade" contracts held up just fine.

The self-doubt didn't seem to show itself to the rest of the world as my colleagues made continuous comments expressing jealousy of my decision. Fortunately there were many months left on my contract during which I would "figure it all out" and they would continue to express their wonder at someone choosing to change her life. June 26th I retired and June 27th I started the process of moving on board Mighty Merry, which was found at that time in Parry Sound, Ontario, Canada, near the 30 Thousand Islands. The farewell parties were over. The "I'm so jealous of you" comments were still ringing in my ears and I contemplated all that had worked itself out in those months from September to June.

Is it any wonder I had gained a bit of confidence? Everything seemed to fall into place with no effort on my part. I had arranged that I would live in the townhouse condo over the winter and in fact wouldn't give it up until after the summer sailing season on the Great Lakes as I didn't want to bother with any of the moving and/or disposal chores during that very brief season.

What a joyous summer. Georgian Bay waters were warmer than anyone could remember so the swimming was exceptional. Gentle breezes all summer long carried me through the intricate waterways of the 30 Thousand Islands down to the bottom of Georgian Bay. Friends arrived all summer for a visit of days or weeks. All had been invited previous years but few had come. They usually had said they should wait until next year but now they recognized there would not be a next year just a day's drive away. Right they were; Mighty Merry would soon be leaving the Sweet Water Sea, Georgian Bay, for saltier water. As I write this many years later I still find my memories of that Sweet Water Sea as warm as from the many salt water seas and oceans I subsequently crossed.

As always during my cruising years in the Great Lakes, I had made many new acquaintances including some who became long time friends. One young couple, Jack and Marianne, became highly influential. They were working extremely hard on the completion of the steel sailboat they had been building over the past several of years. They professed admiration for me in my willingness to set out by myself in these intricate waters while I found myself full of admiration for their willingness to put heart and soul into their dream. I learned that Jack had a bit of salt water sailing experience, and that they had a piece of property on Cortes Island in British Columbia on which they planned to build their dream house. They planned to sail this craft, when completed, out through the St. Lawrence Seaway to Panama, through the Canal, out to Hawaii and up to British Columbia. The diversion to Hawaii is actually the easiest way to get to the northern Pacific harbors due to prevailing winds and currents. We became better acquainted over the summer and considered the idea of me crewing for them from Nova Scotia to Panama. The advantages seemed numerous; I hadn't prepared to leave the Great Lakes as yet and summer was nearing its end, I had little ocean experience and believed I had no business going out on it by myself until I learned more, which that experience should provide.

It wasn't really until then the reality hit me that a decision had been made. I would eventually take my little craft to the ocean by myself and sail it by myself. Why by myself? It was much later before I fully understood my own reasons, but at that moment it came down to the fact that I loved living on board while I didn't believe I could afford to have a home and a boat. A choice had to be made. I didn't really know of any other options; if I were going to live on board as my only home I had best get that home into waters that didn't freeze over every winter. Thus it seemed that another piece of the jig saw puzzle of living with all this freedom fell into place.

The climate in this part of the world is not suitable for living aboard year around. It was already too late in the season for me to depart on my own craft and I wasn't prepared to do so. Additionally I still had to go back to Michigan to move or dispose of my possessions and turn over the condo to the buyer by early November.

Marianne and Jack would be returning to their little cabin up in British Columbia and starting construction of their house, to return in the spring to complete the boat and prepare her to go out the St. Lawrence Seaway. Sometime over the coming winter I would visit them in B.C. The cabin, Marianne said, was smaller than the interior of the sailboat and it would be winter on Cortes Island where they were located. If we could be comfort-able together in those small quarters during the dreary gray days of a British Columbia February we should be able to be compatible at sea.

Part of the childhood dreams I had, which I now realize pushed me in the direction I was heading, had been developed from maps. I had always been a noisy little child and Sunday mornings were torture for me; as the youngest of three children I was obligated to be quiet at all costs while everyone else in the family slept in. (My present husband will tell you I am a noisy gray haired lady as well) Somehow a large atlas had fallen into my hands and at the age of six I had spent hours poring over the intricate coastline of the Inside Passage between Seattle and Alaska while dreaming of visiting that myriad of islands. Now I would actually visit one of those islands and spend a few weeks with people I liked. This was already becoming an adventure!!!!

What about the year in between? I would have no home. Mighty Merry was not in a habitable location and if I thought about it too much it began to be frightening. Well, go do what needed to be done immediately and then stop and figure out the next step. In the meantime start a notebook of lists; lists of what needed to be done, lists of what needed to be learned and even lists of decisions to be made.

The fall colors were developing and the nights were becoming very chilly. Very few sails were to be seen in any direction. The summer sailors' vacations had ended and they were back in the cities earning their keep. I was enjoying myself no less however so it was with great reluctance that I arranged for Mighty Merry's keep over the winter, and prepared to catch the twice weekly bus that ran from Parry Sound to where I had left a vehicle needed to get me and my gear back to Michigan. During the long, slow and bumpy bus ride the solution to the winter began to germinate. I chatted with a stranger in the seat next to me who was eager to share the thoughts from the book he was reading: seeing America by traveling the back roads in a small camper.

So it developed that I sold furniture and household goods and kept my little Honda hatchback in which I stuffed a crate of books, a small one-burner propane fired stove, a tent, my sleeping bag and an exceptionally bright kerosene lantern. Life could never be boring with that much equipment. I would visit the friends in British Columbia but on the way I would see America.

A friend, another Mary, was entering a new stage of her life and decided to join me for a few weeks. Mary, my age and the widowed mother of eight, closed down her insurance business to go back to school to earn a teaching certificate and enter a late career in education as I ended mine but she would have a few months free prior to the beginning of her college career.

We visited a few mutual friends in out of the way places in Kentucky, Tennessee, Georgia, and finally my very elderly mother in Florida. This visit was very satisfying; she was not only approving but thrilled with my plans. Given her experience with a boat and water that seems to me to be an exceptional attitude. Then we wandered along the Gulf Coast until I dropped Mary off at a daughter's house in south Texas and I wandered on visiting my children in other parts of Texas.

I also played a very grand motherly role over those months; both families in Texas were expecting so I made sure I was there for the birth event and to be a helper during those early first days for the new granddaughter and grandson. Fortunately while their births were close together they were far enough apart to allow me to do just that.

We saw Appalachia, the Gulf coast, where I learned how rainy a winter can be and then came Texas via the Farm Market roads. After Texas was New Mexico and Arizona where sometimes I couldn't find any choices to drive other than express ways. I ended up in California. It was a slow trip because almost all along the way there were national parks which I had never visited so I took the time to do so. Next I visited some family members in California and visited the nearby factory where Pacific Seacraft sailboats were built.

By now I realized I had a lot to learn about ocean going sailboats so most of the contents of that crate of books intended to keep me entertained in the lonely evenings related to what I needed to learn. I began to conclude that Mighty Merry did not meet those specifications. One of the few small sailboats that did so were Pacific Seacraft Danas; so, I stopped at the factory and spent a day observing their construction, asking questions and learning the price range and delivery options.

There were other odd things I learned from the travel: such as how to judge how long my forwarded mail would take to reach the next planned destination, how helpful the people in small town post-offices could be, as invariably a conversation developed about how this little gray haired stranger in town happened to be looking for General Delivery mail. I could use that opportunity to make my inquiries about local campgrounds or alternatives. "Didn't I have a dog with me to offer protection," or a gun etc. helped teach me how to maintain a friendly attitude while maintaining a bit of evasiveness. While small town America is very different from a city like Detroit, there are the crazies or angry people everywhere and appearing too naive didn't seem useful.

When did I finally get lonely? It is a vividly clear memory. I had taken route One all the way up the California coast, 101, it's extension, up through Oregon and Washington 'til suddenly I was confronting the salty water called the Strait of Juan de Fuca. I could faintly see Vancouver Island, B.C. from here. It was clearly time to get hold of Jack and Marianne up in BC on their little island and get further directions. This was a complicated process. They didn't have a telephone so first I had to call someone on the island who did have a phone and who was willing to contact them and set up a schedule to meet on that phone. Finally, we communicated. I learned I should take the Port Angeles (where I was) car ferry across to Vancouver Island, drive up to Campbell River, catch the car ferry to Quadra Island, drive across Quadra to the east side, make a phone call from the Quadra inn to get a message to them, and then catch the car ferry to Cortes island. "Remember, the last car ferry to Cortes leaves at 6:00 so you should be able to make it by tomorrow evening. We'll meet the 6:00 ferry." Complicated? Yes, but it turned out to be even more intricate and confusing than the above description.

It was Saturday morning; I looked at my watch. I had mail due at the post office in Port Angeles so I should go first to pick up that mail and then find the ferry schedule. I was in the habit by now of getting all my local information at the post office anyway. My mail was there and I got good directions to the ferry landing and proceeded only to see the ferry pull out just as I pulled into the lane directing me to board. I pulled up to the ticket office and inquired when does the next ferry leave? "Two weeks from today. She's going into dry dock for maintenance." TWO WEEKS. Suddenly I was overwhelmed with homesickness. I wanted to see someone I knew. I wanted to see Marianne and Jack.. At this moment it seemed they were long term friends. I wanted the security of friends. Why was I making this crazy trip? I was almost in tears.

The ticket seller checked his schedule to point out that if I drove fast I could catch the car ferry from Port Townsend to Anacortes where I could catch a ferry to the city of Vancouver, Canada from which I could catch a ferry to Vancouver Island and then proceed on. Ugh!!! It sounded so complicated; which it did turn out to be, but I wanted to get there. Fortunately there weren't any speed traps along that route. When I think back to remember what the road was like between Port Angeles and Port Townsend I am terrified to think about the speeds at which I drove but I caught that ferry (the last one of the day) just before it pulled out.

Driving dangerously fast over a narrow curving road had left me too tired to study the map and understand the complicated route I was taking. The ferry ride was long enough that passengers left their cars for the passenger lounges and the couple sitting next to me engaged me in conversation. They soon explained that I should hope the ferry arrived on time as I had very few minutes to connect with the Vancouver ferry. Very important information, because if I were to miss the Vancouver Ferry it would be a couple days before there would be another one to catch.

It felt so urgent to keep with the plan. Why? The loneliness that had caught up with me? Yes, but also a habit of thinking; the habit I have learned to think of as the American part of me, which says one lays out a plan and sticks to it. Interferences must be forced out of the way; those who do this climb to the top of the heap and those who don't are submerged.

I was left wondering how people living in these places survived the complications of the ferries being their mode of transport from home to work, shopping and taking care of the general business of life. Life would have to be led on such a tight schedule or the alternative of no schedule at all. I could feel the little stress lines around my eyes deepening as I thought of it.

A night in a motel in Vancouver, several more ferry rides, and finally I was on Quadra Island in line for the last ferry to take me to visit my friends. A light snow was falling but melted the minute it hit the ground. While the line had formed to the boarding gate it would be almost an hour before the ferry arrived and I saw people leaving their cars for the coziness of the Quadra Inn and I soon joined them to see the American Super Bowl just starting on the big screen television. The last time I had watched a Super Bowl was in the Pontiac Stadium, ½ mile from my office and it had been 10 degrees Fahrenheit below zero. Right now that one year ago felt like 20 years ago. Still, here I was considerably further north at the same time of year with the temperature not quite freezing.

I pulled out my notes to review the directions to the cabin since there would be no stores or businesses at which to make inquiries once I got off the ferry on Cortes. Since I knew there was no electricity there certainly would not be streetlights to aid me but I needn't have worried. The ferry arrived: foot passengers got off first and there walking directly to my car were Jack and Marianne.

As we crossed the five nautical miles from Quadra to Cortes Island I began to learn about the microclimates that exist from one island to another along this Canadian waterway. The gentle snow changed to a light not very cold rain. Their cabin was built in a rain forest but 25 miles south of us was a desert island; cactus and all. The weather system moved on and the stars and moon emerged to light our way off the ferry and up the winding road to their cabin which was not a great distance away. We turned off the gravel road to a pair of ruts that led to a cozy cabin nestled between the giant cedars on the side of a steep slope. No lights were to be seen except a navigation light in the bay and one at the ferry landing far down the slope. The only electricity on the island came from batteries

We all three laughed with delight. The time and location where we had last been together and planned for this event seemed so far away that it was difficult to bring reality to the moment, but it was time to deal with realistic things since 1, for one, was exhausted and sleep beckoned. I should be shown the route to the outhouse first thing. "Be sure to carry a torch (Canadian for flashlight) in case you run into the bear or the cougar and even though it is winter in the wilds of Canada you will find the seat is warm." All this passed over my head as Jack's typical humor but I followed his directions to assure myself of not getting lost in the forest. A beautiful out- house seems like an incongruity but that's where I found myself. The view was spectacular; there was no door so I could fully appreciate the view. The seat faced a direction from which the wind almost never came and the overhang from the roof extended sufficiently to prevent the rain from coming in. The forest itself provided privacy. One could study the stars at night or look out over the bay by day, and the seat was warm. Modern technology had been applied to one of the most primitive of buildings. Styrofoam instantly reflects body heat.

In all of my innocence it wasn't until my last day on the island that I learned the caution about the bear and the cougar was warranted. A rogue bear had moved to the island and one family actually had moved off the island due to the bear's attacks on their home and cougars did occasionally reside on Cortes. Over the next few weeks I helped pour a foundation for the house to be constructed, we laid plans to meet in Nova Scotia the following October, and I gradually fell in love with the islands and waters of British Columbia. I theorized that if I fell in love with a part of the world during the worst season of its climate, then surely I would enjoy the rest of the seasons there.

The weeks spent with Jack and Marianne were restorative. I found myself spending hours rowing along the tide line in the bays of the island, observing the vast diversity of life, hiking the trails and picking my way across the beach at low tide. Now I had a plan. I would spend the summer cruising one last season in the Great Lakes while selling that craft, would sail on Jack and Marianne's boat from Nova Scotia to Panama, and spend a hurricane season in the Sea of Cortes, Mexico. Then, having had that experience would be ready to take my own little craft on Ocean waters. I not only had a plan but I understood much better what was important to me and I would make it happen!

CHAPTER TWO
THE NEXT STEP

By spring I was back in Ontario. I had spent the winter of 1986 camping, I had visited all the members of my small but far-flung family and I had spent the first few weeks of life with two new grandchildren as well as seeing much of North America and not spending much money. I had, however, committed myself to what felt like an enormous expenditure.

While I remained enthralled by the scenery of our vast continent, I also spent many hours reading and thinking about what type, size and style of a sailboat would best take care of me on an open ocean. I was beginning to realize Mighty Merry, my current craft, did not fully meet my newly established specifications so I took advantage of my time in California to visit Pacific Seacraft to see their boats under construction as well as discuss prices and delivery dates.

Then, while in the Pacific Northwest I had stopped at a dealer and actually sailed my dreamboat on Puget Sound. Believing that I had found the best small boat built for my purposes it probably isn't a surprise that it was the most expensive boat of its size on the market. I searched the country for used Danas for sale. I searched back in California where they were built, in Florida where the availability of used boats is enormous, and throughout the country. The results of my search? Zero.

In the whole USA I couldn't find a single used Dana: a 24-foot cutter rig, designed by Bill Crealock and built by the Pacific Seacraft Corp. The Internet was not yet a common tool. In fact I didn't even know it existed so my search capacity was limited. Very few had already been built at that time: (less than 50) I still believe there were no used ones available. I had succumbed to placing an order for a a new one to be built and delivered to me in Seattle, Washington the first of the coming year, 1988.

I still hadn't figured out how much I needed to live and I didn't have the slightest notion how I was going to pay for this new vessel but that wasn't a problem because at the time I ordered it I had 11 months to figure it out. Why in 11 months I could figure out almost anything. Hadn't I demonstrated that last year? Hadn't I demonstrated that repeatedly in my life? Way back when I was suddenly the primary support of three small children I believed a career in education was the best route for a single parent. Didn't the action I took prove my versatility? I'm quite sure that loan to someone who proved how poor she was could only have been done in a small town bank. A year later a national loan system was set up for helping college students. I unsuccessfully retroactively applied, hoping for the lower interest rate, so I paid the bank's higher interest rate but pay it back I did.

On top of that, the cash deposit placed with the order was so minimal that if I had to back out the loss was insignificant. So the plan was to try to sell Mighty Merry while proceeding out of the Great Lakes towards the Atlantic. This was May and I had until October to meet Jack and Marianne in Newfoundland. The new boat, if I actually carried through and bought it, would be delivered to me in Seattle which brought me close to the waters of British Columbia so it seemed to me I was making great progress in meeting my goals.

In retrospect I must give a lot of credit to Phil Osgood at the dealership. He made a lot of effort to stay in touch with me while I wandered around the 30 Thousand Islands for the next few months. I had no telephone, (cell phones were still unusual and wouldn't have been functional in those remote areas) at that time I didn't know about subscription mail services and I had no long distance radio. I did have lovely summer breezes, warm water and what felt like a lot of time. I still woke up every morning considering myself the luckiest lady in town.

Somehow messages got through to me and we stayed in touch and the midsummer message was that if I could get Mighty Merry to Seattle they would sell it for me with no commission and I would be able to stay in the marina at no charge. I think we both thought that was a bit of a joke given the distance between Georgian Bay, Ontario and Seattle, Washington either by land or sea but the complicated puzzles are the interesting ones.

I was acquainted with some of the Hinterhoehler family, builders of quality Canadian sailboats. One evening in an anchorage somewhere in Georgian Bay, I listened to George Hinterhoehler mulling over his decision to sell his present boat to better represent the company. He would then sail the boat to which they were giving the most publicity. That conversation opened the door for me to inquire about shipping boats cross-country. After all, he built the Hinterhoehler Yachts at Niagara on the Lake, Ontario but sold them all over North America so he had to ship them. He gave me names of several reliable shippers, one in particular who had a yard in the local area and in Vancouver, British Columbia. Apparently owners, dealers and salvage operators shipped lots of boats cross-country. Why not me? Well, the cost was probably prohibitive but the least I could do was inquire. So, with a glass of wine in hand, sitting in front of a lovely bonfire next to a hard piece of granite overlooking the Sweet Water Sea I planned my inquiries.

That inquiry was productive. If I were willing to ship her at the freight operator's convenience the job would be done at reduced rates. His plan was to fill up the truck when he had a shipment going that left room on the truck for my small craft. The definition of his convenience turned out to mean I could pick the week and he would pick the day of the week. To my way of thinking it was very convenient.

By now all my worldly possessions were on Mighty Merry except for my four-wheeled Honda, which had been left back in Detroit with a friend who planned to sell it for me. The same friend also forwarded my mail to me to the various general delivery locations I requested. Now I was wishing it wasn't sold. A quick phone call brought the news that the car market was so bad in Detroit that the big three were selling cars with no interest loans and used cars weren't moving at all. Lady luck was still with me. Once more the carton of books, my tent and the little stove went into the back of the Honda while I watched the crane lift Mighty Merry out of the water and deposit her behind a 40 foot racing machine onto a truck specially designed to haul boats. No matter how many times I have watched my boat come out of the water by crane, travel lift or railway it is always an emotional experience for me and this one was magnified by the distance she was about to travel: from Ontario to Seattle.

Since I was dealing with a Canadian company that had a yard in Vancouver I expected it would be less expensive to ship her to Vancouver so I received a pleasant surprise when I learned that due to the far lower price of fuel in the US as well as the good highways the truck would be going into the US at Sault St. Marie. Thus his route made it convenient to drop Mighty Merry off in Seattle before going back into Canada to Vancouver. My intent was to follow the truck, especially since the driver asked me to be at the Sault when he went through customs. Just in case we lost track of each other he asked me to write up an inventory and leave it with him to present to customs. He also provided me with a toll free phone number to stay in touch with him through the yard from which he came.

I had been living on the US/Canadian border and had been keeping my boat in Canadian waters so I was in the habit of dealing with customs officials on both sides upon entry. But this entry into the US had a slightly different ingredient. Each time a friend or I had come to the boat from the US we had each purchased the maximum allowed in duty free spirits, which was to be consumed while in Canadian waters. Since I wasn't in the habit of drinking anything alcoholic while underway, while alone or at anytime except when well secured in stable weather and sharing the company of friends I had a sizeable supply remaining. In addition of course were all the rest of my possessions; a reasonably well equipped galley, my clothing, normal toilet supplies, books, charts etc. etc. Normally I would have listed those in exactly that manner. The liquor however presented a special situation since it was supposed to have been consumed while in Canadian waters and customs had every right to confiscate it when I passed back into the USA. I wanted to be cooperative and informative with customs but also I didn't want to give up the liquor supply. Equally I didn't want to lie so I developed a technique I have subsequently used with customs officials all over the world. If one were to lie and be discovered the consequences can be dire; confiscation of not only the object but also the boat, my only home, as well. On the other hand most of us are aware that customs officers frequently seem arbitrary so after while it feels like playing a game.

My technique? I went through the time consuming task of handwriting a complete and highly detailed list of every item on board and its location, which resulted in four pages, two columns each page HAND WRITTEN. (Not particularly good quality handwriting either.) In the middle was listed: "various open and unopened bottles of liquor under the galley sink, behind the cleaning supplies." The key here was handwritten and the quantity of handwritten items. I didn't generalize; every single item was listed.

Upon delivery in Seattle I inquired how customs had reacted to my inventory. His body language told the story best. He grinned from ear to ear, shook his head while his whole body shook with laughter and said "Lady, he took one look at that list, shook his head and waved me on." This exercise taught me a great deal which I subsequently utilized in many countries. The minute detail of the list gave the appearance of honesty, (which I was) and for many customs officers reading it would require more effort than they were willing to expend. In some instances the officer didn't even read highly legible English, let alone when written in my scrawl. At least I can say that I never had Mighty Merry Too's contents ransacked while many cruisers have reported experiencing just that. There were also occasions when I had experienced gentle seas before arriving so I baked a few peanut butter cookies to offer as refreshments to the visiting bureaucrats. American cigarettes and/or liquor are often offered by other cruisers but that was against my budget and/or principles.

I was about to set out for the Sault after making a few phone calls when I discovered there was one more detail back in Michigan that needed a personal appearance to be solved. Would the tentacles never be all cut free? After a hasty trip through Detroit and suburbs I was finally ready to head west. Believing that the truck had to be through Customs at the Sault by now it, seemed practical to take the southern route around Lake Michigan and up to the highways leading West through Wisconsin, Minnesota, the Dakotas, Montana, Idaho and Washington. Perhaps we would find each other once on the highway in Wisconsin or Minnesota. The advantage to this route, in my opinion, was that I had never before traveled most of it so it would be a sight seeing adventure.

When I was near the Wisconsin/Illinois border I called to find that I was ahead of the truck so I could plan on a leisurely trip. As the trip proceeded I experienced lovely early fall weather and campgrounds were easy to find and almost deserted. The nights were chilly enough I headed for the nearest warm restaurant for the morning cup of coffee but the further west I got the clearer the skies seemed to be until one memorable night in Montana when I just didn't want to go to sleep for star watching.

While at this moment I don't have the slightest idea where in Montana I was, I do remember the road which seemed to stretch as a long flat ribbon and as endless as Texas had been when suddenly a mountain loomed straight ahead up out of the flat land. The road curved around the lower edge and I came across a café, motel and campground on a lovely stream that seemed to wind around the base of the mountain. While not yet dark the almost full moon was already coming up over the eastern horizon. I treated myself to a good meal, (at an amazingly low price), and thought about a motel room until I took a look at the moon and star filled sky and pitched my little tent down near the gurgling stream. My decisions to camp were often influenced by the fact camping was a significant economy measure but frequently just the beauty of my surroundings enticed me. I was soon asleep but wakened, chilled to the bone, very early but after moon set, to see the most spectacular star filled sky I had ever seen. Now I understood why they call Montana "Big Sky."

I arrived in Seattle several days ahead of Mighty Merry and walked into the dealership to announce the fact that she was on her way to be sold by them as offered on the phone. Tom Cooper, the Pacific Seacraft dealer gulped with a bit of surprise and welcomed me. After discovering my mode of travel cross-country he arranged for me to stay at the prettiest campground I have ever seen before or since, near La Conner.

Labor Day weekend was coming up and I expected it to be crowded but the few people there were all huddled together, mostly in big travel vans, in one corner near the showers, television room and such facilities while I had my choice of all the rest which provided as much privacy as a person could want. I had been in the habit of pitching my tent in state and county public campgrounds across the country, which frequently had minimal to no facilities so I would occasionally take a motel room for a night to have the luxury of a shower and perhaps laundry facilities. This was a whole different milieu. It apparently was one facility out of a chain across the US and Canada and most definitely was set up for luxury semi-outdoor living. one had to buy a membership to use the campgrounds. A guest status had been arranged for me but I definitely was an outsider. The concept of a tent seemed to be a startling innovation but I was out of the way and inconspicuous which I preferred while I savored the sense of adventure I was feeling.

Several times, as I was driving those thousands of miles between Penetanguishene, Ontario and Seattle, I asked myself out loud: "Do you really think you know what you are doing, Mary? You are going to a big city where you don't know anybody, you are having a boat built you haven't figured out how to pay for, and you expect to sail in waters full of rocks, and ferocious currents when the only ocean experience you have is sailing to the Bahamas with a guy who wouldn't even let you row the dinghy."

Then some other memories came flooding back. Why, just a few weeks ago, when being forced to come into a dock under sail in unfavorable conditions, the skipper of a commercial dive boat came over to compliment you on how cool, calm, and collected you were when you went on the rocks coming down to Bouselei Island. Yes, but you did go on the rocks. Yes, but you did get out of that predicament with no damage. Yes, and you did get through the predicament of losing the gearshift cable. Yes, and you are 57 years old and free from responsibility to anyone but yourself so if you get into trouble you get yourself out of it and live with the results. Or if you don't get yourself out of it you still live with the results. Isn't that better than not doing?

Thus I defined my future: move on towards adventure and live with the results.

So there I was in Seattle four months prior to the expected delivery of "the perfect boat" for my purposes with no idea of how I was going to pay for it. The first step I needed to accomplish was to sell my current little craft, which should at least make a down payment. Once I had sold her, it seemed to me, I should be able to obtain financing for the balance. I actually needed to accomplish the first step pretty promptly since the factory wouldn't start construction without a sizeable chunk of green in their hands.

My mobile life style presented another problem: my mail. This was before the days of e-mail and cell phones were expensive and uncommon. Aside from convenience there are numerous reasons I absolutely needed a mailing address and I really did not want to lay that responsibility on my children. They lead busy lives and even were I to pay them for doing the service it would have been an intrusion on their lives. Additionally I would feel reluctant to complain or criticize the quality of their service. While at the campground at La Conner I had come across a magazine aimed at people traveling in RV's, in which I came across an ad for a mail service. I saw this as a whole new and very useful concept. For a small monthly fee I would have a mailing address, a toll free telephone number to call and arrange for mail and phone messages to be sent as I moved around. Based in a small Oregon town the service was initiated by a widow with young children who had found a way to have a business at home. I admired her initiative and the service seemed like the perfect solution for me.

One example of the convenience of it all: Federal documentation of a boat serves much like a car title or property title for real estate. It is an absolutely necessary item when entering a foreign country but one has to have a mailing address to obtain documentation. I was able to use the mail service for this purpose as well as for taxes and other such obligations.

Over the years I developed a great deal of fondness for Shirley, the woman who ran the mail service. It wasn't until she sold the service ten plus years later that I understood what quality service she provided and how rock bottom her rates really were. As is so often the case, we don't appreciate what we have until we are forced into a comparison.

The amazing part of all this convenience is that the US Post Office frowns on these businesses; at least that is what their behavior teaches me. I can't really imagine why, since they receive postage on every item twice rather than just once. They proved it to me however when at one point in my travels I received a packet of mail including a demand from the post office: that demand required me to complete a detailed questionnaire, have it notarized, and then return it. If not completed within such and such a date Shirley would not be allowed to forward my mail to me. I repeat; she paid new postage every time she sent my mail. Not only did I feel the US post office had infringed on my rights and privacy they cost me an arm and a leg. I paid a taxi $50 US dollars to get to the US consulate in that country and then the notary charged me $75 for performing the service of watching me sign a document, checking my identification, and then stamping and signing it herself. She proceeded to read the entire document: I proceeded to point out to her that there was no necessity for that. In fact, I reminded her she had no right to do it. I had been a notary myself and knew what I was talking about this time.

But here I was in Seattle where I had found that the boat I had brought all the way across country didn't have a big market. It had been built on the east coast and had a good reputation there but the name was unknown here on the Pacific Coast. Only days before the deadline for getting the down payment to the builder Lady Luck did come smiling; a potential purchaser finally came to look at Mighty Merry. It does only take one person looking if it is the right person; he was.

I was also glad to be able to say I was pleased to see him as the owner of my treasured craft even if he did split my lip open. I was demonstrating the idiosyncrasies of the little Honda engine, pointing out that starting the engine required almost no effort. He either didn't hear me or didn't believe me because he pulled with great but unnecessary effort. I'm sure you have experienced something of this sort. You pull hard; it comes free so all that effort throws you off balance and who knows what come next. In this instance what came next was his elbow to my lower lip, which was split wide open and required several stitches. He did take me to the emergency room for care at the nearby hospital. I assume he enjoyed the boat because in 1998, more than ten years later, I happened to be in Seattle and saw he still had it; she was for sale again however, since he was off in Africa on a photographic expedition.

We had agreed on a price and I had his payment in my hands just in time to get the first part of the down payment to the builders of the Dana before the deadline. There was a waiting list for building these sturdy little craft so if I lost my place in line it would be a year before I could be in the same position.

I rented a storage locker in which to place my worldly possessions as I removed them from Mighty Merry and turned her over to the new owner. Now I didn't even have that little wee home but I did learn that the builder would allow me to watch the construction of my new little sailing home. To my fascination, they let me in to the construction to observe.

The carpenter offered to come to the boat and add any details I might want if I were to sail her down to California. Additionally, I felt even more confident when I learned that the salesman who sold me the vessel was also having one built for himself. Thus I watched the two craft being built side by side. When the holidays drew close I visited my far flung family so that I arrived back in Seattle on New Year's Eve. Mighty Merry Too had been completed and launched into Lake Union without my presence.

She was properly christened as *Mighty Merry Too* by Phil Osgood. I just didn't feel like Might Merry II described her well enough, although again I had chosen a name difficult for people in other cultures and my own culture to grasp.

New Year's Day dawned as a beautifully clear and sunny day but brisk; quite counter to all I had always heard about gloomy Seattle. It was late in the day when we were ready to step the mast, which would allow me entrance in and out of the cabin, but we managed it just as the sun was setting. We had just proven another advantage to this small craft; the mast could be stepped without the use of a crane. In this instance two young men and one small woman accomplished it.

Now I could move my possession on board. While I wouldn't be able to sail her until the instruments were mounted and activated I could begin to turn her into my home. For that matter there was a lot to learn before moving out of the slip even into little Lake Union which connects Seattle to the Strait of Juan de Fuca via a pair of locks.

The diesel engine is an example of my ignorance. It is much more useful than the gasoline outboard motor I had always used to get around in tight places where one couldn't depend on wind and sail but, I knew nothing of the use and care. While Lake Union was a small lake it was extremely busy with both pleasure boaters and commercial aircraft. I knew enough to know there was a lot I didn't know.

Part of the economy of Seattle seemed to be teaching classes related to cruising, both coastal and overseas. I began to take classes; navigation and use of the sextant, diesel engine maintenance, preparation for a ham radio license and even usage and maintenance of 12 volt batteries as well as measuring usage.

My confidence was vastly boosted by all these classes; at least I knew the questions to ask as well as where to turn for more information when needed. Additionally, those classes increased the profits for a number of Seattle vendors as I purchased and installed what I came to believe was essential equipment for a small ocean going craft. GPS wasn't available then, although Loran C was, so it seemed appropriate to buy a good sextant. I passed the examination for the lowest level ham radio license so then of course I bought a ham radio even though I really didn't know how to use it. Then I had to have the proper antennae taken to and up the backstay. Radar sounded useful but even with the solar panels I did buy, radar seemed to me to require too much electricity. Hah, already those classes are paying off. More knowledge helped in the decision making.

As I write this chapter today I have to work hard to remember how I perceived my plans at the time I retired. Experience has since taught me that I could travel and see the world on what most Americans would call a shoe string when I brought my home with me and chose not to be encumbered with too many bulky possessions. I also gained freedom of choice regarding time. Back then I think I thought of this plan as traveling to Canada and probably down to Mexico but I wasn't picturing myself as crossing three oceans.

I was also learning my way around Seattle. I parked my car in a different neighborhood every day, studied the map and marked off a route approximately 8 — 10 miles and walked. This was my routine almost daily from New Years until I departed for British Columbia a few months later.

I suppose there was a certain amount of "contagion" going on here; i.e. I was spending a lot of time with and around people preparing and making plans for long ocean cruises on their sailboats; all of them larger but not necessarily more sea worthy than mine Many of them were less sea worthy in my opinion then and in my opinion many years and three oceans later. Since I was already a bit used to being an unconventional person it was not a case of just following the crowd. We're talking about a life style and the pursuit of an activity I knew I enjoyed so it was easy to be encouraged and to let my planning move in that direction. There were a lot of aspects somewhat in conflict with my preferences; i.e. I'm not crazy about the tropics but I do love to snorkel in warm coral waters. I enjoy brisk weather but get worn out easily in hot humid weather. Most of these boats were planning to head to the tropics where the trade winds blow and it is never cold.

Well, no sense in worrying about all of that. Even if I were outfitted for a world cruise my thoughts still said "all I'm planning at the moment is to go north to British Columbia to visit those waters I had enjoyed so much when I visited Jack and Marianne."

Oh, speaking of Jack and Marianne; what happened to that trip where I was going to crew for them? I was to meet them in Newfoundland and accompany them to Mexico, or Panama. I would gain all this experience. Well, they got to Newfoundland and decided they liked being on their island in BC better than they liked sailing to get to it so they sold the boat and returned to their island. By the time I received that news I was so happily into my project that I wasn't the least bit upset over that interruption of plans. The biggest disadvantage to not doing so was that the time period spent crewing was going to be a time period when I wouldn't be spending any money but whoops; here I was spending money every time I turned around and mostly for some very expensive items. Also it was mostly money I didn't have so the charge cards were doing duty. I was well equipped however.

I still had that automobile that didn't sell back in Detroit a year earlier; it had served me well and now it was suddenly a burden to be gotten rid of. Much to my surprise, despite the 100,000 miles on the odometer, I got rid of it for almost the price I had paid for it several years before. So, for the first time in 38 years I didn't own a car and it was with great pleasure that I looked forward to a life with no car and no telephone. Today, many years later I still consider two of my greatest luxuries to be categorized by lack of ownership; no car and no telephone. (Well, I'm cheating just a little. I'm in South Africa as I write this chapter and do have a cheap cell phone that gets turned off much of the time and nobody has the number to call me.)

Finally one day I was ready to leave. I started north and stopped in lots of little and large ports along the way. I quickly learned where the shipping lanes were as there was constant traffic of ships from all over the world, especially Japan. Sailboats have the right of way over power boats in most waters but do not have the right of way in the shipping lanes; those giant monsters do. Everything was a day sail and everything was different from the Great Lakes and a major adventure. In my life adventure only comes in one style: major. Some are of longer duration but if it is new it is an adventure and this was new. I had the right charts, guide books, tide tables and current charts with me: I had learned how to use them but psychologically I really wasn't prepared for what I saw when I looked at the first pass I needed to traverse. Granted it wasn't time to enter; I knew I needed to wait for slack water; that time period when the tide changes and for a brief time there is no real current. However the rushing water told my senses that that pass was filled with rocks. All of my Georgian Bay experiences told me there were rocks, rocks and more rocks there and if I went through that pass there would be no more Mighty Merry Too.

Well, the guidebook and the charts said otherwise. The current charts and tide table told me that if I would just wait it out all that rushing roaring water would abate in about an hour and turn to a smooth quiet narrow opening leading into a wider body of water. I watched and waited. Before it actually quieted down I saw a fishing trawler enter and go right over those rocks with nary a sign of difficulty and no additional noise. Hmmmmmm. My watch finally told me it was time to enter and lo and behold; no sign of those rocks anywhere. The tide tables and current charts were correct; I could and did safely move right on through to the body of water that would lead me to the San Juan Islands. That ferocious current I had read about and had just seen demonstrated really did stop when the tide stopped flowing in preparation for a change of direction. So, I had proved to myself that I had learned some things correctly. Thus I determined I could certainly afford to continue on.

I often wonder at a fact which I have learned from listening to people talk about me when they didn't know I was listening. Doing so with others unaware is very easy to do on the ham radio where there is free and easy communication to nearby and distant places but absolutely no privacy. For some reason I became a topic of conversation across the airwaves which led me to wonder at the fact that I can feel so inadequate and self questioning inside when those around me see me as exuding confidence. I later learned that one local man even blamed me for his divorce when his wife felt confident enough to leave him. I didn't know either one nor any of the story that led up to it.

That self confident appearance isn't a put on in that I'm not trying to show anything in particular but I do know that how I feel is very much a result of what I consciously or unconsciously tell myself. If I feel I'm facing a predicament it is self destructive to tell myself negative things such as, I'm in trouble now, I don't know what to do, or this could be the end etc etc. When I'm feeling very hollow inside, my mouth is dry, and perhaps my hands are shaking; it is time to consciously talk to myself. Maybe I can define the problem out loud because with a definition some answers will come, maybe ask myself enough questions that I lead myself to some answers, but whatever I tell myself I can't afford for it to be negative or threatening in any way. Even if it is no more than a postponement, i.e. I'll think about that later when I have more information, or after I've had some food and am refreshed etc. A postponement is better than a negative. Telling myself a negative becomes almost like a whirlpool that sucks me in and the next statement will be more negative until I'm sucked right into the maelstrom.

I learned that process a long time ago while suffering some really deep, lengthy, and debilitating depressions. It sounds like such a trite and Pollyanna behavioral explanation but conscious thought can lead to emotional reactions that overcome the emotions resulting from unconscious thoughts. I have often puzzled over why the unconscious thoughts, in my instance at least, are so negative and therefore destructive. As early on in my adventure as at this stage I heard people talking about me in a manner as though I were doing something extraordinary. I thought then, and I think now, that I was conscious of what was necessary to do in order to do what I wanted to do. I had learned in those painful days of emotional depression a very helpful tool many people could utilize.

But here I was finally starting the adventure for which I had spent so many months preparing. By now I was beginning to think and talk in terms of heading south to California and then on to Mexico but not until I had spent a summer season in British Columbia; testing out the equipment, testing my own skills with the equipment but mostly just plain enjoying myself and enjoy myself I did.

The scenery continuously overwhelmed me; there were times when I could see both Mt. Rainier and Mt. Baker. While the waters were not the clear blue of the famous tropical islands they were teeming with fish, crab and prawns as well as mussels and clams along shore. I soon became quite expert at clam digging, mussel picking, setting my crab trap and hauling up the catch. At times the easiest thing to fix for breakfast was another crab. Just haul up the trap set the evening before and pick one out to steam. To haul up an empty crab trap was a rare event. I've also subsequently learned that I much prefer the seafood from those cold waters than that from warmer waters.

There were stupendous waterfalls, huge rocky bluffs with variegated outcrops of different rock and ancient shells deeply embedded. The growth was quite totally different than I had known in the Midwest so it was another learning experience to name the trees, the wild flowers, and the myriad wild herbs and berries. Each island tended to have a personality of its own, due often to the different climactic conditions and soil. All of this is still a wonder to me today.

That first season I had no plan; I simply wandered from one sheltered anchorage to another. My choice was based on wind direction that day and what I heard from other boats about a particular location or what I read in a guidebook. Most of the people I met were local and had a lot to offer in the way of information about the local area: best anchorage, where some of the wild delicacies were to be found, how to differentiate a male and female crab (only the males were legal to keep) as well as the easiest and tastiest way to clean and cook a fish or crab etc. Quite contrary to New England lore the local method was to kill and clean the crab before steaming it and I still agree with that choice. I might have been influenced by the fact I really couldn't' carry a pot larger enough to cook a live crab. The locals had no interest in gathering and eating mussels, which simply left the lot to me as well as the recent European immigrants. We found them very tasty and they were that much more plentiful for the lack of local interest. Additionally the waters were clean and we didn't have to worry about pollution causing the toxic problems found in mussels and clams in the more populated waters.

Much of the area I visited was Provincial Park land; there were no roads leading into this area so it was very much still in its natural state and felt primeval. As I studied my charts I continued to marvel that here I was in the part of the world I had spent so much childhood time dreaming about. Not only that but it matched the beauty of my dreams. The previous winter I had read a book written in the depression era about a woman who had taken her children by boat through these waters every summer season for a number of years. Now that I was doing it myself the major regret I had was that I hadn't done that with my children who were now far too busy with their careers and family to even come visit me.

I had always heard about the rain and gloom of this part of the continent but my experience just doesn't agree with that description. I will grant you that it wasn't a great area for swimming and snorkeling but I had day after day of sunshine and gentle winds. As the weeks progressed into fall I enjoyed it even more; there were no more wild berries but still plenty of fish and seafood and wild greens. The evenings were cool enough it was a good time to bake that loaf of bread as the oven would heat up the cabin while providing a nourishing and tasty treat to accompany a bowl of fish chowder. By now I had started a batch of sourdough starter so to keep it going and usable I baked a loaf of sourdough every third day; the weather was cool enough it needed most of the day to raise after mixing it in the morning and I enjoyed the warmth from the oven in the evening.

Didn't I miss television and all the other modern conveniences? In a word; NO. If there were any earths shattering events that one really should know I would hear about them on the ham radio.

I did learn a bit more about my personal reaction to our modern environment. I had been in the habit of always having good music around me; my radio tuned to Public radio or a record or tape player providing my choice in music but always something. I had a good radio and tape player (CD's weren't as commonly around yet) with very good speakers but I found I only played them when I wanted to consciously listen to music. I enjoyed the silence in between, perhaps because it wasn't always silence. I was listening to the birds and learning to identify at least some of them by their song as well as all the other sounds of nature.

My last five summers had been spent cruising the waters of Ontario; some of it with purpose to get from here to there or to meet a guest or to show my grandson new vistas but most of it was simply to experience the day. It was now spring, almost summer and while I had a general idea of some places I would like to go (certainly Cortes Island) I was prepared for a season of going where the wind took me much the same way as I had enjoyed in the Great Lakes.

While I enjoyed a few days at Anacortes my impression of the San Juans were beautiful islands that were too well populated for my preferences. I soon moved on to cross the border into British Columbia. At Bedwell Harbor, Pender Island where I first met Pete and Doris, the couple who would eventually own Mighty Merry Too. We cleared customs almost simultaneously and found in common our interest in small boats. They were sailing Tan Barque, their little Flicka, built by the same builders as my Mighty Merry Too.

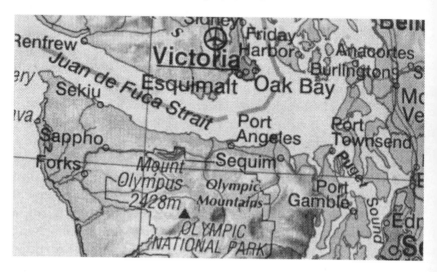

Clearing customs and immigration wasn't quite as easy as it had been in when entering Ontario on the Great Lakes. Still it was easier than about any place else in the world I've been since, which is a lot of countries and continents. I did learn that I was pretty free to roam Canadian Waters for the next six months although I would have to report at the end of that time. I really didn't realize what a luxury that was until moving further away in the world where often one is required to clear in all over again with every movement within the country.

I had been in touch with my mail service so today I picked up mail at the local post office This was almost always a rewarding experience since it was before the days of the much faster e-mail (before e-mail for me at least). Before I had an opportunity to row my dinghy home to Mighty Merry Too and peruse my sizeable package of mail I made the acquaintance of quite a variety of people. Throughout the world post offices have become the most common place I've first met the locals of small towns. In many countries everyone picked up their mail at the post office since delivery service was often non-existent or very unreliable.

The first person I met was the nurse who ran the local medical clinic which only occasionally was visited by a doctor. I was quite taken aback by her all embracing, "Oh, we love you crazy Americans. It allows us to be ourselves; to each other we're so stodgy." Gulp. Should I be complimented or insulted. Well why be either? Enjoy; which was exactly how I proceeded.

Then I met John V. who lived on his boat wherever he happened to be and sometimes worked and sometimes lived off the land. In the next few months I met a significant number of people who lived off the land. He thought I might like to meet the American woman who had recently moved here; she happened to be from the same immediate area from which I came and she introduced me to her South African partner. He had fled South Africa some years before as crew on a sailboat. The captain of that sailboat had been a woman. Even though white, he had created a problem for himself as an opponent to apartheid and so sought and gained asylum in Canada. Through the years I met a number of South Africans with a similar attitude and experience.

The result of seeking my mail was therefore a very sociable half-day and by the time I rowed home I was quite surprised to see a significant portion of the Canadian Navy at anchor in the bay. Little Tan Barque was gone already but I simply had too many invitations from locals to move on so swiftly and I suspected I could learn a lot about some of my intended destinations from some of these people and I had no deadlines after all.

Canadian Naval Vessels

In the mail bundle I received a letter from high school classmates reminding me that tonight was the beginning of a weekend of get togethers celebrating the 40th anniversary of our graduation. I had earlier decided that it would be great fun to join them but then I also began to think about the fact that since I had not seen most of them since that graduation why would I interrupt this adventure of a lifetime to fly back to Michigan to join them? Since the group with whom I had been the closest was getting together for a dinner this evening I could easily arrange to call them, which I did do. I really found myself quite curious as I thought about it but after the conversation I was very glad to have spent the money on a phone call rather than a plane ticket. Much of the time on the phone was spent listening to a man who now lived in Southern Illinois and who had never been on a sail boat in his life. He gave me much advice based on what he knew of his neighbor who was building an ocean going craft in his back yard. I found myself puzzling over the fact that so often the people who know the least about a particular subject are the ones to give the most advice about it? I didn't know the answer then and I still don't but I still believe the truth of the statement.

When I finally lifted anchor a few days later to continue on it was with a lot more information and even more anticipation for the beauty lying ahead of me. I stopped next at Beaumont Marine Park; a popular anchorage and like so many of these little harbors it was a Canadian National Marine Park. These marine parks were often inaccessible in any manner except by boat and frequently there were facilities to dump ones garbage, get fresh water and sometimes there were even toilet and shower facilities.

I did have my own homemade solution to the problems of taking a shower on board. I filled a garden sprayer, which utilized a hand pump to build pressure, filled it with warm fresh water and used it in the head in an area designed for a more standard shower. I had been using that system on my previous boat and realized the significant advantage it gave in controlling the usage of fresh water and electricity. I hadn't worried much about controlling fresh water in the Great Lakes but my shower system had been useful there as well. It was easy enough to heat the water over the flame on my gas cook stove.

Speaking of garbage, away from land I feel free to dump anything biodegradable overboard. What doesn't simply rot deep underwater probably gets eaten by one of the various salt water residents but close to shore there is the danger of the incoming tide carrying it up to the beach and creating an unsightly as well as stinky mess. More difficult is the disposal of plastics and it is very difficult to shop in any supermarket in any country without coming home with a lot of plastics.

I hadn't had the anchor down long when my VHF radio blasted out "Hello, Mighty Merry Too. Please come join us for a crab dinner. We're the power boat just ahead of your anchor." I looked up and could see there were already a large number of people milling about on board so I realized it was a quite general invitation but I couldn't help but think, "These Canadians sure are friendly." Upon arriving I promptly received an open bottle of beer and while I was being introduced around someone commented about the power boat at anchor on the other side; it seemed to contain a lone man, quite elderly who didn't appear to have a dinghy and he didn't respond to a radio call but they would certainly like to invite him as well so I did volunteer to dinghy over, relay the invitation and offer a ride.

As I neared the boat a large bushy and very noisy dog greeted me. I wasn't sure if it were a greeting or warning but the owner came out shushed the dog and accepted the invitation. He was Roger, long ago retired from the Canadian Navy as a hydro graphics specialist and taking what he saw as his last trip on his little craft. His family (children) had objected to his doing so due to his age: 80. Further I learned that his real dream was to go to Princess Louisa Inlet since it had been his first project as a hydro graphical specialist. Well, Princess Louisa Inlet was all I had been hearing about for the last many days. I had no real notion what it was really about because I had no real notion what any of these spectacular islands, passages, anchorages and state and national parks were about except for Cortes Island which I had visited.

So far I had learned that when I saw an island on a chart that appeared by latitude and longitude to about the size of an island I was used to seeing back in Ontario as thus and so it appeared to be enormously larger when I came up to it on my wee craft. Now my craft wasn't all that much smaller than what I had sailed in Ontario so what was I missing? My imagination just wasn't hitting on the height when I studied the charts. These lofty craggy islands were much larger if one included the height of the mountainous terrain in contrast to the rocky high hills of the Ontario cruising grounds.

My friend Helen used to sail with me frequently on the Great Lakes. She is an artist and taught art. I have long recognized that I have an extremely poor sense of spatial relations and that is an aptitude taken for granted in an artist. In the days we sailed together I was acutely aware that she always identified where we were. Eyeball did it for her before chart plotting except for the one foggy day when I had to come through with chart plotting. Back with Helen eyeball told me almost everything, or rather told her and then she told me but Helen wasn't with me any more. Now I had to rely entirely on my navigation skills and eyeball just wasn't going to tell me a thing. I shall never get over the feeling that I would love to have those skills because I still come in to every port wondering if I can really believe what I see. I don't in fact, but I do believe what I have plotted on the chart so I am continually in awe of what appears before me; all of it a complete surprise.

If anyone reads this who has the good fortune to have some navigation experience and a good sense of spatial relations I know that shivers are going down your spine as you realize what I am saying or perhaps more to the point as you realize what I see and don't see. But somehow I've made it; more than once, across three oceans, a few seas and from island to island to island and through those coral reefs as well.

The other thing I was learning was that there were a lot of marvelous and edible living things lying about in these waters just waiting for my crab trap or fishing line and it was obvious these people around me had a lot to teach me about accessing this very tasty food source.

But back to Roger and his desire to revisit the spot where he had started his career a good many years previous. After I learned just how long the distance of Jervis inlet, the fjord leading to the waterfalls and anchorage of Princess Louisa inlet was, I recognized his problem; he simply didn't carry enough fuel for his powerboat nor did he feel he had the stamina to handle his craft through 46 miles of rocky coast as well as the strong tidal currents to be met. I soon realized it was certainly on my list of spots I would like to visit as well so finally, after many hints and finally a direct request I agreed to take him to Princess Louisa on my little craft. Only after I agreed to do that did the issue of the dog come up. I like dogs but dogs do not belong on a small sailboat. I question if they belong on any boat but it was clear that the minimum time for the trip was two days and that didn't allow for any time spent admiring the scenery and water falls after arrival. What was to be done with the dog if he didn't come along? Thus ultimately I agreed to Roger and his dog.

I suppose I should have anticipated that in 1988 an 80-year-old man would very likely not have confidence in a woman's ability to handle a boat; but I wasn't prepared for a lot of things resulting from that trip, included among them the fact that by the time the sun had fully risen (we left at first light) Roger was giving me orders on how to sail the boat, despite the fact he said he had never been on a sailboat before. Since he had drawn the original chart for the area I was willing to listen to navigation advice but not sailing advice.

We agreed the dog would remain in the cockpit and a stack of newspapers were brought along since it was trained to use the newspapers much as I remember having puppies do. The distance to the head of the inlet was equal to a comfortable days sail if we had sufficient wind but for most of the distance there were high cliffs on each side so it was doubtful we could hope for consistent wind. The current would be with us half the trip and against us the other half. There was no place to anchor along the way: i.e. the water was much too deep and the bottom rocky. There were plenty of hazards en route as there are in all these waters. Most frequent among the hazards are enormous floating logs. With all those cautions in mind I didn't really want to travel after dark. Therefore whenever our speed went below a certain point I added a few rpms on the motor to what the wind gave us so we arrived in plenty of time.

As we circled around at our destination looking for the best anchorage I was confused and puzzled as one Canadian after another shouted, as their greeting, "Happy Birthday." After a dozen or more "Happy Birthdays" Roger answered my puzzlement. "They noted your American Flag. It's the Fourth of July, your Independence Day. Ours was a few days ago, on July 1st." I was truly delighted by that bit of friendliness. It was a gesture I had never experienced before or since and will long remember.

There was a long single dock along one wall of the cliff, intended for small craft to use but it was filled up with boats. Before I settled on an anchorage a fish boat moved off his section of the dock and signaled to me the availability of the space. With a dog on board my immediate thought was what a blessing.

Roger suggested that he take the dinghy and go catch us a fish. I suggested to myself I would just wander around and take in the spectacle of waterfalls and rock cliffs surrounding us. I could see Roger a short distance away and gasped in wonder when he pulled up a fish large enough for two dinners. My gasp turned into a scream when a seal leaped up and grabbed it right off Roger's hook. The scream changed to convulsive laughter, which was quickly echoed from the other boats. Roger moved further out, beyond hearing distance, and threw the line back in to try again.

I returned to Mighty Merry Too and indignation. As I prepared to step on deck I was confronted by a growling, snarling and very ferocious looking dog. I remember uttering an "Oh shit. This dog now believes this is Roger's new boat and he is the guard on duty. So I gotta wait 'til Roger catches a fish." So, I sat down on the dock and the dog and I glared at each other, much to the amusement of our neighbors, one of whom came over and handed me an opened and well chilled bottle of beer and inquired how long my father had had this boat. We were soon joined by most of the dock residents and as I told the story the laughter became so uproarious that I was forced to see the humor also but was delighted when Roger finally came home with a substantial catch which was more than tasty after a few minutes on the barbecue.

The scenery was magnificent, especially the water falls and well worth the trip. I vowed I would return before leaving British Columbia for good. After getting Roger and his dog back to his vessel a few days later I spent a glorious summer wandering from one lovely anchorage to another. I became skilled at catching crabs, picking oysters, digging clams as well as catching fish. I also learned just how abundant they all were.

JERVIS INLET TO PRINCESS LOUISA AND THE PARK

FALLS

One of my favorite memories is the retired butcher from the Kootneys, an area of British Columbia. He and his wife literally lived off the land. Their sailboat was very old but large by my standards and they had amazing equipment on board. I was served beer he had brewed on board, mushrooms they had picked, bread baked in the oven of the massive old cast iron wood stove that was both a heater and cooker. The wood he had cut on shore and/or picked up drifting. There were jars and jars of venison from the deer he had legally shot, butchered and then preserved as well as blackberry jam and I can't remember all the other goodies but I do remember a sense of awe at their self sufficiency. They stated their only food purchases were flour and sugar. They too were German immigrants who came here shortly after WW II. They talked about the fact they had urged their relatives back in Germany to come join them in this land of plenty but to their surprise, as well as disappointment, none of them ever had.

As the summer waned the anchorages became emptier and emptier and I enjoyed myself that much more. The summer holiday sailors were back in Vancouver, Victoria and Seattle while a scattered few of us liveaboards were finding fall every bit as nice as summer with the exception of the reduced hours of daylight. I was considering spending the winter when I received a message indicating a family in Seattle was interested in hiring a crew to navigate for them on a passage between Seattle and California and I had been recommended. Would I be interested? Well, it would help replace all that money I had spent outfitting Mighty Merry and it would also provide an opportunity for an offshore passage; an experience I believed I needed before setting out on my own.

Thus, I headed south to Seattle, met the family and looked at the boat. We discussed equipment and planning. The decision that we weren't suited to each other was probably simultaneous but I saw a whole lot of things wrong with the project including the fact that the boat wouldn't be ready until so late in the season that I would expect one storm after another coming down out of Alaska. I later learned that the broker delivered the boat for them but within a few months after their arrival in California the boat was up for sale as they found themselves unsuited to the lifestyle. But now I was back in Seattle. I had heard so many stories about how bad the weather is in Seattle but I hadn't seen much evidence of it. True, I had been gone November and December the previous year but I had seen little but cool sunny days from New Year's Day forward until I saw warm sunny days and now again there were cool sunny days. More than a decade later I will state that whatever the weather in a particular place is reputed to be it seems I see and experience something different. As I write this I am supposed to be experiencing lots of rain and occasionally some very violent storms but actually we are experiencing a drought.

I began to think however that I would like to fly back east and visit my family; my mother was in her early 90's and still living independently and I particularly wanted to spend some time with her. I had lots of photos to show of my summer journey and she was a wonderful audience. I do so remember one of her comments; "one of the few regrets I have in life is that I can't spend just one morning having my morning coffee and watch the sunrise in your cockpit." That was also the visit when she warned me; "Just you remember this: don't you dare come back here for a funeral. If you do I'll come back and haunt you." I saw her two more times. Three years later while sitting in an anchorage in Costa Rica I received a message via the ham radio that she had died. I received that message within ten minutes of the time my brother had called my ham friend to pass that news on and I was warned once more that she had not wanted me to interrupt my journeys for a funeral. Minutes before hand I had turned down an invitation to join a group for drinks and a dinner on shore; I changed my mind and joined the group long enough to offer a toast to my mother to whom I owe so much.

CHAPTER THREE
THE THRILL OF SEEING SEA LIFE

I was eager, after my summer season spent in British Columbia, to see more of that same part of the world before continuing on to more distant destinations. To this day I can say that I gained so much satisfaction from what I experienced in those waters that if I had never gotten to the tropical blue waters of the South Pacific I would feel all my efforts at obtaining, outfitting and preparing this little craft would have been well rewarded. When I set out this time however, I set out with a plan that would allow me to venture into more beauty and at times more challenge.

I would revisit those spots I considered especially rewarding; continue on to the top of Vancouver Island, then on to the Queen Charlotte Islands which would take me almost to the entrance to Alaska. From there I would return to Port Townsend on the Strait of Juan de Fuca in order to prepare to head south to California and ultimately Mexico. My return route would be very different as I would come down the West side of Vancouver Island; where I could expect far fewer visiting boats but also could expect the terrain to be far less disturbed. The plan included arriving back in Port Townsend in time to make preparations for a California departure before the fall storms settled in.

What did that require in terms of timing? There were many infrequently visited but very sheltered harbors on that West side so I certainly wanted at least four or five months to explore many of them. Let's work backwards. Dig out the pilot charts for that part of the Pacific ocean so I could see what the winds are like in the autumn months heading from Washington State to California. The pilot charts would not necessarily predict but would tell me the wind conditions for each month in the past over a very long period of time. If the winds were favorable 90% of the time from September first until the 21st over the past ten years for instance and the other 10% were not extremely unfavorable then the odds were very good for that time period. My study led me to believe I should leave for Caliornia by mid to late August. I'll want to spend one to two weeks time in a port with available supplies and shelter for preparation. Well, that sounds like I should leave for BC by March or April. Isn't that pretty early?

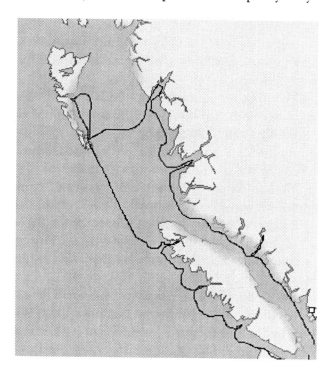

OUTLINE OF ROUTE FROM SEATTLE TO QUEEN CHARLOTTE ISLANDS, BC

Back to the pilot charts and to the Canadian Pilot, this also gave a great deal of information. It had been a much colder winter in Puget Sound than I had experienced the previous winter so to someone from Michigan it did sound pretty early. When I discussed it with other cruisers and wannabes in the marina, they all thought it sounded much too early. Still, when I looked at the averages from previous years it looked like I actually should be underway by April 1st so I decided to go with the real experts who put together the Canadian Pilot rather than the conventional wisdom from other boaters all around me.

The strongest motivation of all was the history of less fog in those early months. As I traveled north I would often be in very narrow bodies of water with rocky areas on both sides of me so fog was an even worse hazard then it might have been far out at sea. I didn't have radar and didn't see it as a practical addition on my little craft.

I did depart late March and spent most of April enjoying the same area I had so loved last year, only this season I enjoyed it even more for a variety of reason. While I kept hearing about how bad the weather was on shore, just a mile or two off shore it was just fine with much better winds than last year. I admit to feeling a bit smug over my timing decision. To my delight almost nobody else was in the areas that had been downright crowded last year.

Also it was a bit like that last season in Georgian Bay; friends flew in from Michigan to join me as well as friends from Puget Sound. Just getting to our meeting point was an adventure for most of them because they had to make their way to little known and hard to reach locations, but as one of them commented: "Where you go, Mary, seems to be among the most beautiful places in the world." If I were to make the same trip again I would follow the same schedule. I checked in on the ham nets with regularity where I listened to people talking about the foul weather they were having several weeks travel behind me while I experienced lovely winds with cool but sunny weather. My ham radio license was still quite restrictive until I could pass the Morse Code test but I could listen in to what I needed most; which was weather conditions in different areas. The ham nets were simply a group of people who checked in each day at the same time on the same radio frequency; usually there was a leader who was sort of in charge. I saw almost no fog, which is a frequent event and is the most discussed weather phenomenon of the area.

My arrival seemed a surprise to the marina wharfingers; Canadian for dock master. One wharfinger remembered me from the previous year and he pointed out there was no point in paying fees until departure time. He then commented that since it was Friday afternoon and he was going to take the weekend off he was pretty sure that "anyone with the kind of heart you have Mary, will be gone before I get back Monday morning. If there is nobody here to pay you can't very well pay can you?" The only other vessels present were commercial fishing boats. They offered me a choice from their hold for dinner.

As I reminisce today I think of my friend Peg and I back up at Princess Louisa where we were by ourselves except for the day when a small seaplane came in with a group of tourists for a quick look. Last year there had been a magnificent waterfall and so many visiting boats it was difficult to find a safe anchorage or spot at the one dock. This year there was a magnificent waterfall along with hundreds of other smaller ones roaring all around us. The mountaintops were still all white as well.

Last year I did not pick oysters because it was too late in the season for them to be safe to eat but this year we ate oysters to our hearts content; clean, plentiful and so very tasty. No shucking them; just pop them on the gas barbie at the stern and they quickly pop open. Drop the crab trap and it was invariably full when I pulled it back up. At one point Peg wanted to take a photo of the pile of oyster shells. I resisted that with the awareness that I never wanted anyone to see what a pig I had made of myself. Today, I wish I had that memento.

We did have a few other visitors; a seal came in and grabbed a fish right off the hook as it was being reeled in: a reminder of last season's trip with Roger. We also saw bears on land across the bay. They were close enough to be interesting to watch but far enough away to not feel threatening as there were some enormous waterfalls between them and us. We had so much privacy that we took our showers right out on the dock using the same garden sprayer I described earlier. It provided several advantages. One of the most significant was that it gave me control of how much fresh water guests used since fresh water is always at a premium on a small boat. What is conservative usage to land people seems outrageous to those of us on such small vessels. It is far easier and less irritating to control the usage than to preach about it.

One of the really favorable characteristics of these waters is the lack of biting insects. If there is a mosquito or sand fly etc. in the area it will find me and have a good meal and I will itch unmercifully for 35 days after. In these two seasons of travel I only found one port, Powell River, where there were mosquitoes and I never found sand flies. Years later in New Zealand's Fiordland which compares very much to this BC area except even less populated, the sand flies were a constant nuisance. They were so incessant that I wore a home made bee keeper hat at all times while the rest of my body was always completely covered for protection at any time outside the cabin. Even though we had equal privacy I didn't take showers outside on deck or on the dock there.

I had gone into Vancouver to pick Peg up but dropped her off at a harbor that at least had roads coming in to it which meant there would be a bus to take her back to Vancouver but she was on her own to find it. Like me, she isn't afraid to ask questions of strangers and in those remote areas people are eager to be helpful. That's the only kind of guest I was willing to invite because I didn't feel I had the time to shepherd them to and from their home destinations.

I then continued on north toward the Queen Charlottes which meant traversing waters which were entirely new to me. It also meant I would be going through one of the most notorious passes in this part of the Canadian Inside Passage. The tides are extreme with the result that when the waters narrow the currents become ferocious; the one I'm thinking of here gets up to 12 knots so even fish boats with very powerful engines wait for slack water. The waterway is narrow because the rocky slopes have converged on both sides so if a skipper loses control they will be thrown against those rocky walls which will destroy almost any boat. I will guarantee that in a 12 knot current you will lose control. So what is to be done? Wait for slack water, which occurs when the tides reverse. That provides a quiet period of about 10- -20 minutes. A least now I believed it would happen in contrast to my fist traverse of such a pass. Never were the tide tables more important to me than for getting through these passes. Of course I can see when it is slack water but I also needed to plan ahead since it happens only once every 6 hours; safe anchorages are sometimes a full day's travel from one to the next. These waters are absolutely unsafe for travel after dark due to all the huge floating logs. Thus, if I were to lose several hours waiting for the tides to change I just might be in a trap.

Jan, who owned her own sail boat, joined me next with the primary goal of seeing whales since we were in the territory where the Orcas lived and traveled. Orcas are frequently called Killer whales because they are the oceans greatest predators. Like wolves they hunt cooperatively. There are resident Orcas that remain in certain waters and are well identified and named by those studying these magnificent creatures. There are also transient pods, which regularly travel through these waters, back and forth from north to south and return. I was just as eager to see them. Additionally there are off shore pods that occasionally visit so it seemed our odds of seeing them should be pretty good

We were greeted with friendship at every port along the way. At Alert Bay, Grant Barker, the ferry driver, gave us his car keys saying that he would be gone all day driving the ferry and we should have the opportunity to drive around the island sight seeing. We stopped at Port McNeil, a port up close to the top of Vancouver Island, at the time of a halibut opening. An opening is the brief time period the commercial fishermen with halibut fishing license are allowed to fish.

This time period might be weeks, days or even such a brief time as hours. We had walked a few miles from where we were moored when we came across a fish buying and processing plant. We stopped to watch a fish boat unloading the catch of these giant finned creatures. If the grin on the face of the boat's owner was a measure of the quality and size of the catch then it was a good season. While the heads contain the cheeks, the tastiest part of the fish, they are obviously not practical for processing for the big markets so the heads were being cut off and thrown aside. We happily assented when the fisherman asked if we wanted some heads. We departed with three heads, one in Jan's large black garbage bag and two in mine. We quickly learned to appreciate just how huge a halibut can be when those three heads turned our brisk walk into a slow and then even slower trudge before we got them home, but get them home we did. Actually they provided food for several days.

In Puget Sound and the Gulf Islands I had seen dolphins, which are actually small whales, which had coloring similar to Orcas. At first I thought they were Orcas as did some local long-term residents I had met. Even though the Orcas are no where near the largest whale they are the greatest predator whale. I still had not seen these giants however so Jan and I were both keeping an eagle eye look out. These creatures are now being studied intensely, but until quite recently little was known about them and the "common knowledge" was often erroneous. Dolphins of all types are always welcome visitors but we both longed to see these giant creatures in their natural habitat.

Jan stayed with me as we made our way through a number of different rapids: Yaculta, Dent, and Greenespoint, timing each entrance with slack water. Despite our watchfulness we never did see Orcas while she was with me but we did see bald eagles all along our route. I wrote in my journal one evening, that we had seen more eagles than we could count. I still laugh out loud when I remember how entertaining they were. It was spring and evidently it was the courting season. For some reason they seemed to be particularly numerous in the areas where we waited for slack water. I suppose fish were more visible in the quieter waters and thus easier to catch. If I understood what I was seeing it would appear there were more males than females as in each instance we saw several eagles showing off to a rather complacent eagle while the showoffs were highly aggressive to each other. While we didn't see nests right here I did see many nests a few weeks later. Before departure from British Columbia I began to see the young ones learning to fly and hunt for themselves. Later, when I was on the West side of Vancouver Island, the residents puzzled over us considering them a protected species since in their eyes there were so many Bald Eagles that they were a nuisance. All young pets (kittens, pups etc) needed protection from them so they didn't become dinner.

Unfortunately Jan didn't continue on to the Queen Charlottes so she never got to see the whales from the cockpit of Mighty Merry Too. She stayed with me in the Inside Passage to Shearwater, just around the bend from Bella Bella; an Indian settlement. There was a government dock at Bella Bella but the village itself was an enormous disappointment since the store was poorly stocked, not very clean and the village itself was equally not very clean despite the fact the houses were all very very new. The Canadian government had recently come to a financial settlement with this group of Indians and they apparently used the funds to build new houses. Too bad they didn't maintain them. We ate dinner in a restaurant in Bella Bella and have no other description for it except awful: almost inedible.

Just around the bend we found Shearwater, a great contrast to Bella Bella as it was extraordinarily clean. Commercial transportation in the form of a seaplane came and went, a marine store offered supplies to the fishing fleet, docks for visiting vessels and even a very good restaurant.

I had my first encounter with the Canadian Coast Guard here at the dock at Shearwater when their ship, Racer, came in. The wharfinger informed me that Racer needed the particular space I was in for reasons I no longer remember, although they seemed perfectly reasonable at the time. I offered to move immediately since absolutely every other space was empty. He quickly admonished me to just stay put because the Coast Guard would do all the work of moving me. Indeed a few minutes later I was gently pulled into a new spot; all my lines properly and efficiently retied and then offered a loaf of fresh warm bread straight from the Racer's oven. Ordinarily I wouldn't let someone else tie my lines but if I couldn't trust them to do it properly who could I trust? Later when my friend Sue arrived on one of the seaplanes we were given a tour of the ship. I saw Racer again several times while up in the Charlottes and was always offered a friendly greeting.

Sue's first view of the local wild life was upon our return to Mighty Merry Too when we found numerous little dark furry creatures running around the decks: mink. Fortunately I had left the cabin securely closed. It was a bit unnerving but they left with little prompting and I was reassured by the locals that with humans on board they would not return.

Our plan was to depart from here to the Queen Charlottes which meant we would leave the sheltered Inside Passage route to Alaska to cross Hecate Strait. The Inside Passage weaves between hundreds of islands and mostly rocky, mountainous shore. Sue, an accomplished sailor, had come especially for this part of the trip having never been to this extraordinary group of islands.

The archipelago is mostly a protected National Park administered by the Haida Indians, the original inhabitants, in conjunction with the Canadian Park Service. It is theorized that this group of 160 plus islands missed the last ice age and therefore life developed differently from the coast only 60 miles across Hecate Strait. The largest Black bears in the world are to be found here along with tiny deer and an abundance of plant life different from that found anywhere else. The abundance and variety of birds includes the largest population of bald eagles other than Alaska. The fish population is highly varied and plentiful as is the seafood. The diversity of intertidal life provided another path to investigate. With 23-foot tides there is a wide stretch of beach to explore at low tide.

The waters can be treacherous as well. Strong currents pushed us around. Many of the protected areas that would make superb anchorages are unusable because the water is extremely deep and often the bottom is rocky rather than sandy or muddy so anchorage could be iffy at best. I knew if I could get an anchor to hold on a rock the likelihood is I would never get it back up. I used to experience similar situations up in Ontario waters but back in Ontario I didn't go up and down with the tide so I could frequently tie to trees along shore. This just doesn't work with these enormous tides unless you are willing to continuously watch and change the lines every time they become too loose or too taut as the tide goes out or comes in.

The fish population made it attractive to the Japanese so early that they charted the waters of the islands before the Canadian government did so. I saw pictures in a museum of the Japanese fishing fleet taken shortly before World War II. It did give me pause to realize how close Japan is to us in this part of the world. Back in Michigan on Pearl Harbor Day the Japanese had seemed a world away.

The rain forest on the island chain, like the coastal rainforest from where I was departing, contains the densest biomass in the world; greater than the tropical rain forests.

The passage across to the Queen Charlottes was delightfully uneventful although it didn't really go quite as planned. A commercial fish boat came in to Shearwater and they advised us of a very sheltered anchorage, Rudolph Bay, on the west side of the large island from which we would depart to cross Hecate Strait. We saw this as leaving from the closest point and thus we should be able to make the crossing entirely by daylight. While we had no chart covering it, his directions were so detailed it seemed to both of us we would have no trouble finding it. Thus we planned to use it as the spot to deflate the dinghy and bring it on deck and just generally prepare for a crossing of Hecate Strait.

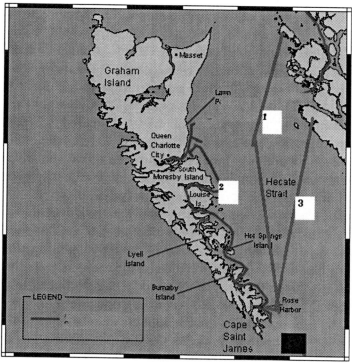

ROUTE FROM INSIDE PASSAGE TO QC 1
AREAS VISITED 2
ROUTE TO VANCOUVER ISLAND 3

We were dead wrong! We found an entrance at the location he gave but it was nothing I was willing to enter. Actually Sue went in by dinghy to test it out a little more thoroughly and came back even surer it was no place for us due to the rocks littering the bottom. We really felt ourselves to be in a pickle since it was too late in the day to go back to the original plan We finally faced up to the fact our only choice was to cross Hecate Strait at night. We both stood watch all night scanning for the probable logs ahead of and around us. We were most relieved to not hit any of the many enormous logs floating around in those waters, which could have made the crossing very eventful. We breathed a sigh of relief as daylight broke just as we neared the islands. It was late enough in the season the nights were very short at this latitude.

NAVIGATION CHART OF IMMEDIATE AREA

There were three cabins at the head of Rose Bay where we entered. Before I could get the hook down the owner of the nearest one came out by dinghy and offered very welcome advice. The fishing boat on one of the buoys was his, but the other buoy was provided by the Canadian government and intended for commercial fishing boats but I was welcome to use it. It was also advisable to do so since the bottom was very rocky and unsuitable for anchoring. I normally won't tie on to an unknown buoy because of my uncertainty of its condition but with his reassurance it seemed the safer thing to do. When a fish buyer came in and needed the mooring he tied Mighty Merry off from his side and then invited me to dinner.. The moorings were put there by the government for the safety of the many commercial fish boats that came to this area from the mainland.

A local resident,(the only one resident at the time) John Weir, brought a welcoming gift as well; a huge piece of fresh halibut. To this day really fresh halibut is my favorite fish but I am spoiled by the quality of what I had up there. He also invited us to visit their home at our leisure. He told me the story of his very first halibut catch: it was so large he couldn't get it aboard the fish boat he had then so he dragged it to a very small island where he pulled it up to butcher it. I've had very few fish since to compare to the taste of those British Columbia halibut.

Sue was to be with me for only a brief time before flying back to the mainland to her boat brokerage business. To make use of her brief time we quite shortly set off to explore the area between here and the location where she was to meet the seaplane to take her back to the mainland. After her departure I returned to Rose Bay and several times visited the family living here: John, Susan, and their two young sons. He was a biologist from Indiana. After coming to Canada he obtained a commercial fishing license which was their source of income. His wife was from New York City, the child of a Jewish immigrant family who had survived the holocaust. Her parents simply could not grasp why she wanted to be living in such an isolated area. The two young sons' academic education was home school.

Further, I was invited into their garden to pick fresh vegetables as desired. While it still seemed early in the season in such a northern latitude the garden was lush; I had forgotten what these long hours of sunshine could do for the growth of greens etc. I did get a chuckle out of the fact they had no television (what lucky parents) but the boys did have a computer. The Honda generator was run almost every day to provide the electricity for them to work on computer projects. No, they didn't have access to the internet.

Nothing I had read before hand had exaggerated the magnificence of the Queen Charlottes. I was enchanted by the rain forest and eager to go for a hike through the giant cedars. It was particularly inviting because there didn't appear to be the mass of undergrowth that normally blocks one's way in a rain forest. Then I took my first step and sank up to my knees in the dense moss. By now I had several local guides who led to me to ancient totems, a canoe high up in cedars, which had been the Haida's traditional practice of disposing of their dead. I was also shown the most convenient beds of seafood. These guides were actually the two young boys being brought up in this isolated area. I have no question in my mind about the future attitudes of these young boys: two of our more ardent conservationists.

As I had made my way north the only vessels I met other than commercial fishing boats were three large sailboats outfitted as tour boats: Darwin Sound, Maple Leaf and Island Roamer. The opportunity to talk to the captains and crew of these boats was very beneficial as they were well acquainted with the waters and climate to which we were headed. Once up in the Charlottes they provided some real treats. After all they were advertising their trips as "adventure tours" and playing up the hazards to be confronted ahead. Their guests arrived by seaplane. They also were treating their high paying guests to what might be expected in the way of fine food and wine considering the tariffs for these trips. The result of all this was that once there, if I happened to be in the same anchorage I was treated as an honored guest. The paying guests were guided to a view of wonder and respect for this little gray haired lady sailing these treacherous waters by herself in a vessel that truly did appear minuscule next to their sumptuous craft. Although it felt a bit overdone I was able to put up with this fawning attitude while partaking of gourmet meals accompanied by a fine glass of wine. While I found the fare aboard MM Too perfectly appealing to my taste it was also great fun to be indulged by someone else's efforts. One boat in particular I remember had originally been owned by the "Galloping Gourmet" of television fame and had a particularly well equipped galley and the cook on board was doing it justice.

The sight that most stands out in my memory was a lovely afternoon sailing in an unusually wide expanse towards a new anchorage when nearby I suddenly saw a large pod of Orcas frolicking; I was totally enchanted and let MM Too wander rather freely as long as the Orcas stayed in view when suddenly a new wonder popped up from immediately under the bow; *a huge humpback whale had been swimming right under Mighty Merry and surfaced at the bow.* Had I been at the bow instead of the cockpit I could almost have touched the tail. My heart stopped momentarily and then began to pound and continued doing so for almost an hour as I contemplated how easily that giant could have simply destroyed my little craft.

In subsequent years I have met two couples whose boats were destroyed by whales. Both were wood boats in contrast to fiberglass. One of the theories I have heard theories expounded is that they don't attack fiberglass boats but I've heard no real evidence to back that up. I also knew a couple whose steel boat hit a sleeping whale in the Tasman

Sea. That whale then sounded and immediately departed but they spent a number of nervous hours waiting for it to return and attack them which it never did. They also spent a good deal of time recovering from the stench resulting from when it blew.

I was shown many gestures of friendship while in the Charlottes. At one point I was in Queen Charlotte city (a town of about 940 people) at the government dock. As in most Canadian waters the government provides marinas, usually well maintained and always reasonably priced, even for a foreign guest. The wharfinger introduced me to a gentleman who handed me his car keys, saying, "I heard that you wanted to drive up to Masset. I drive the ferry to the mainland and don't need my car today or tomorrow so if you would be so kind as to drop me off at home you are welcome to my car." The offered loan of the car was a repeat performance of friendship as that similar instance had happened down in Port McNeil, almost at the top of Vancouver Island.

Masset is the largest city of the Charlottes, (1500 people) and there was a German couple living up there on their boat, Vagant. I had hoped to visit them and indeed did. They also found the local people very generous. Vagant had been dismasted and the locals helped them find a cedar adequate to replace their mast, helped them fell it and provided tools for turning it into a mast and stepping it. It was a year's project but it got them going again and I met them many years later in New Zealand at a time when I was recovering from damage and injuries.

While the Haida, the Queen Charlotte natives and original settlers of the islands, are not always welcoming to Caucasian strangers I received an invitation directly from the Chief to visit their headquarters. (I was told it was out of respect for my willingness to sail to reach here.) There were countless other gestures of kindness I experienced.

When the white man first came to the New World the Haida had been one of the most prosperous of the indigenous peoples of North America. Making a living was sufficiently easy for them that they had time for elaborate art work and festivities. They were renowned seamen; using their huge war canoes to travel south, often to capture slaves to do their work for them. I had discussions with several locals over their observations that individual Haida seemed to have little initiative or apparent ambition but when numbers of them got together and worked as a group they seemed to work together unusually well.

I didn't really feel ready to move on but I realized it was time to do so since I still planned to travel south to California and there was much to still see on the west side of Vancouver Island before doing so. I do get to choose what I want to do and when I want to do it but Mother Nature often interferes with the "when". The west side of Vancouver Island is another area frequented by fish boats, only a few tourists who mostly came in by air to fish and/or hike and canoe but very few cruisers except way down at the bottom at Barclay Sound. Even there few Seattle or Puget Sound sailors visit. It appeared to me that more Oregon cruisers came to Barclay Sound then either Canadian or Washington cruisers, most probably because the Straits of Georgia were a very convenient and attractive cruising ground for both Vancouver and Washington residents as they were more accessible to people who had brief vacations for cruising. Oregonians had little in the way of good cruising grounds until they got up to Barclay Sound which made them much more adventuresome sailors.

A spurt of bad weather greeted me just when I was prepared to depart. I was back down in Rose Harbor where I had first entered, tied on to a mooring and simply waiting for a weather change when I heard the Canadian Coast Guard calling "pan pan pan, Mighty Merry Too." I was more than startled since the pan pan indicated an emergency of some kind. It must be that a friend was in trouble because I certainly wasn't. I responded immediately, only to learn that people up in Prince Rupert, closer to Alaska via the Inside Passage. had become worried about me since I hadn't been on the radio for some time. A call to the Coast Guard resulted in a search for me. This wasn't the last time this sort of thing occurred.

When the weather pattern changed to more favorable conditions I departed early morning to cross Queen Charlotte Straight for Quatsino Sound on the northwest side of Vancouver Island, expecting it to be a 30 hour plus passage. The days were now very long in this northern summer; but it wasn't until I made this passage that I realized just how long. In most anchorages I had had high mountains surrounding me, still snow covered, so I was quite enchanted by the fact that once at sea the sun never completely set. It lay very low on the horizon while the full moon rose and the sun remained on the horizon all night until it rose high in the sky the next morning. It was my first and only view of the midnight sun and it was a breathtaking sight. It was only then that I put into perspective just how far north I had gone. Queen Charlotte City is at 53 degrees of latitude N while Cape Horn is at about 50 degrees latitude S. We all think of Cape Horn pretty extreme to the south. Alaska is to the East of the northern part of the archipelago.

My first visit on the west side of Vancouver Island took me into Quatsino Sound a very protected body of water varying from 1 to 7 miles wide but 50 miles long containing towns and villages. I made my first landing at Winter Harbor which boasted a population of 20. Despite the small population this snug little port boasts a well built and well maintained government dock which is well utilized primarily by commercial fish boats. At that time the only access was by water or seaplane but today they brag about access by logging roads which are usually a pair of ruts.

I remember this landing with a good bit of embarrassment because frankly I was rather rude to the gentleman who met my little craft. He was eager to take lines. There was one fish boat at the dock and a little tiny vessel that appeared to me to be almost a toy even compared to little MM Too. As was my habit; I had a line on the midship cleat and brought back to the cockpit so I could ease Mighty Merry up to the dock (where there was plenty of space) and simply step off with that one line, secure it and then secure the forward and aft lines. The boat couldn't drift too far away for the dock for me to step back on board which might happen if I had used either a forward or aft cleat.

A man came from the "toy" craft and tried to help with lines, inquired about where I had come from and all the usual niceties. I was less than appreciative of his offer of help since I always redo the lines after someone else does them for me. I simply want to be sure they are well secured.

After realizing that I had been sailing for about 36 hours he promptly invited me to dinner on board his craft stating he had a very nice piece of fish he had purchased from the fish boat across from me as well as a respectable bottle of white wine. I couldn't imagine how this was all going to happen on the "toy" boat but I was tired and it all sounded appetizing and he really was very gracious. Additionally my curiosity got the better of me so I promptly accepted and in retrospect was so glad that I had. Here was a true adventurer: he was circumnavigating Vancouver Island on this little craft. I no longer have the details on the dimension etc. but it was approximately a 10 or 12-foot sloop with a tiny outboard, very shallow draft especially since in place of a keel there was a retractable centerboard. He pointed out that he considered himself safer on it than I would be on Mighty Merry since, in the event of a sudden change of weather, he could simply beach his craft and wait out the storm. Actually he was making a camping trip around the island.

He had built it himself and thus was fully acquainted with every inch of it in the event of anything going wrong. The cabin was really tiny with merely sitting headroom. He had already eaten his dinner (he said) and served mine on the table that was only large enough to serve one person. A few weeks later I learned from other sources that he was a very wealthy Vancouver businessman who owned several very large craft, one sail and one power but chose this for the pure adventure it offered.

I was soon ready to move on to where I would meet my next guest, Mary, when lo and behold on a mooring in a tiny cove along the way was a boat I recognized from back in the Seattle area. When I called on the VHF radio to say hello the response to my greeting was: "You are the hardest person in the world to find. I've been looking for you for weeks. Everyone I talked to recognizes who you are.,knows you've been there, but nobody knew where you were going next. Let's buddy boat." My response was that I'd be happy to share a big fish I had on board if he felt like cooking. I figured this would give me time to think this through since I normally am not keen on the idea of "buddy boating" and I was even less keen on the idea after I did try it out with him some weeks later.

The first impediment to his suggestion was timing since I would be waiting for Mary. We would spend at least a week together here in this lovely inlet where there were many smaller inlets and bays as well as two small towns, both with a lot of history. For Mary a big part of the adventure was simply getting to the small town where I would meet her. It required multiple flights to get from Detroit Metro airport to Victoria but then the fun began. First a bus up the east coast of Vancouver Island to the point where she could catch the twice weekly mail truck that carried a few passengers via logging roads to Coal Harbor, the most inland of the towns on this side of Vancouver Island. Mary is the friend who had accompanied me on the motor trip that first winter of my retirement. The entrance to the more northerly bay where Coal Harbor lay was one of those small passes where the ferocious currents flowed so once more timing was very important.

Just south of that pass lay the village of Quatsino where there was a machine shop which I needed. I had heard about it from the fish boat back in Winter Harbor but had not yet found it and realized I really didn't have time to stop or I might not be up in Coal Harbor when Mary arrived. I considered it highly inconsiderate to not be there considering the distance she was traveling to join me and indeed I was there.at Coal Harbor when she arrived. Her arrival was luckily timed so that we could almost immediately get back to that ferocious pass through which I came to get to Coal Harbor during the one slack water that would be during daylight hours.

Our first venture was back to the village of Quatsino where we had heard of a very fine restaurant that served only local catch fish and seafood, vegetables all grown in their own organic gardens as well as a fine wine selection. The fact that it was also within my budget was equally attractive. I insisted on being the hostess when guests were with me for several reasons. If they went to so much trouble to get to me it seemed the right thing to do. Additionally I had been advised that if ever anything went wrong and I had allowed a guest to pay for the slightest thing I could be sued as a "tour" boat and any insurance I had would be void.

We had just been served a glass of wine with hors d'oeuvres when a large man in work clothes came in asking for me, in a very gruff voice. I was more than startled but I did respond to discover that he was the owner of the machine shop I had planned to visit. We were given evidence of just how small and integrated these communities are as he explained he had heard I was in need his services but he was closing up shop for good that very same day so if it was important to me I had best get it done right now. I did need him, and although our order had already been placed the owner interceded to say there was no problem holding it back so off we went with him. Despite the gruff voice he was very helpful. While unable to do exactly what I wanted due to lack of parts he was very able to improvise a solution that lasted for many years.

I have developed a great deal of admiration for craftsmen of his type. We learned a bit about his history as he proceeded with the job. He had come to Quatsino sound on holiday thirty years previously, fell in love with the area and never left. I also heard from him how "ridiculous (in his eyes) the US was about protecting the bald eagles." Just look around you; they are nesting all over and there isn't a chicken or small animal safe from them." I had been fascinated by them all the way up from Port Townsend and I am still happy to see them protected.

After exploring the Sound a little further we sailed over to Port Alice at the southwest end of the Sound where we ended up docking at the local Yacht Club. At the restaurant in Quatsino we had been invited to the Club and given a code to get in and out of the gate. On our way I set a prawn trap, which was a whole new venture. I had been warned to set it at least 50 feet deep, which was far different from the way I used a crab trap. The plan was to pull it up when we departed Port Alice. Mary and I left the Club for a long exploratory walk. When we returned we found a huge full gunnysack in the cockpit: so big in fact that I had to stand on tiptoe to see inside once I opened it. I gasped as I looked at the contents; a huge supply of giant prawns. Mary cried, "what are you going to do with those?" Why eat them of course, after a few minutes on the gas barbie that is. Eat them we did and enjoyed every single one, which stuffed us for several meals. I never learned who the donor was but that person knew more than I did about setting prawn traps because mine was empty when we retrieved it a few days later.

After Mary's departure I met up with my friend who wanted to buddy boat. He had been patiently waiting for me to make up my mind and let him know and I really couldn't think of a reason not to do so. I suggested let's get a weather report and plan our departure time. While waiting for me, he had drawn up a set of 20 alternative plans to utilize in the event we ran into trouble. He pointed out that like most capes our trip past the Cape Cook would be fraught with danger and we should be prepared and remember, "You're on the west side of Vancouver Island where all those ferocious storms come all the way across the Pacific Ocean." Well, I do believe in being prepared but 20 alternative plans sounded to me like overdoing it just a bit. In fact, in an emergency how would one choose between them? As it turned out our trip past Cape Cook was completely without wind and we had to motor most of the way. Once more I had a deadline to meet in that

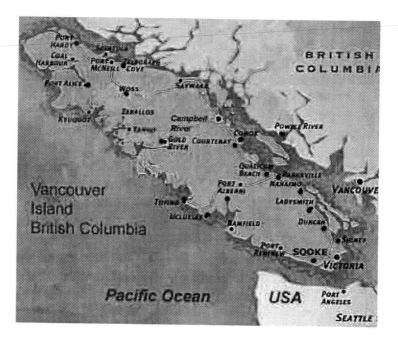

I had more guests coming to meet me in Tofino. The closer we got to Nootka Sound the more we saw of civilization; for instance a *floating bookstore*. The owner pointed out that she only carried "good quality books", "none of the trashy stuff. Some of the fish boats (her primary audience after all) want me to carry detective stories and romance novels but I won't do it." She was too far northwest for very many tourists to find her so I guess the fish boats got culture whether they wanted it or not.

My next guests, my long time friend Diane and Don, her now husband, would meet me in Tofino. The various inlets, bays and coves between Quatsino Sound and Nootka and Barclay Sound were extraordinary for the sea life, shore life, and just the natural beauty of an area that was a little too remote for commerce to have intruded. Weeks later when I was preparing to head south to California I was torn because I really hadn't had enough of this beautiful area but I also realized that I was no spring chicken and there was still a lot of the world I wanted to see. My friends who met me in Tofino probably said it best. "Mary, when Diane said you had invited us I wasn't sure if this would be worth my two weeks vacation but I have to tell you, just the first six hours would have been worth the whole trip." His wife, Diane is the Diane who spent the summer with me way back when I had broken my hand.

So finally, in August I returned to Port Townsend to prepare Mighty Merry Too for the off shore trip from Washington to San Francisco, California.

MARY AND GRANDAUGHTER KATHRYN
I DID SAY I'M A SHORT GRAY HAIRED LADY

CHAPTER FOUR
DISTANCE TRAVEL BEGINS

I returned to Port Townsend to prepare to sail to San Francisco which means I cleaned and shopped. I found MM Too was still in good condition; her bottom was still clean enough for months more of travel, engine oil changed, hoses all inspected, and I had gone up the mast to inspect everything up there and on the way down. Charts, food, and spare parts headed the purchase list.

I did end up with crew; Brian and Joy, a couple from Nanaimo that I had met cruising up in British Columbia. They were planning to do the same trip in a few years and wanted the experience of off shore travel so they met me in Port Townsend. They had a lovely cruising boat of their own where they lived each summer and I had spent time with them in a variety of BC anchorages. We three seemed compatible; although three was a large number of people for this small craft it also seemed rather sensible for this type of trip.

I utilized every inch of storage space; several inches of space under the cabin sole was the coolest place on the boat so our many small cartons of fruit flavored yogurt were placed there. Fresh fruit and vegetables were hanging from nets in a variety of locations We joked about the fact that if the Coasties (US COAST GUARD) should board us all those little cartons under the sole would be highly suspicious since in that era the only thing the Coast Guard inspectors were looking for was drug smuggling.

The US Coast Guard did board us in the Strait of Juan de Fuca It was quite a revelation to my Canadian crew who were quite amazed to see them with guns on both hips. hey approached us in a high-speed rubber ducky and requested we maintain course and speed as they came along side and stepped aboard. They were highly efficient and courteous however and they posed no problem since we, after all, didn't pose a problem to them. I didn't feel the same the next time they boarded me almost a year later between San Francisco and Mexico.

We sailed the first leg of our trip through the Strait of Juan de Fuca to Neah Bay, a Native American settlement right at the very most northwestern tip of Washington. This would be our only port before San Francisco. Both ports are notorious for plenty of fog. My plan was to head west about 400 miles, which would take us out past the continental shelf and most traffic; once we were out to what I thought of as safety we would head south. Most of the shipping traffic stayed pretty close to the coast as did most cruisers. The latter usually stayed 50 to 60 miles off shore with the view that if NOA reports indicate the weather will turn bad they will head in to the nearest port. I guess this is just fine if you have enough speed to get into shelter before the bad weather hits but I didn't believe I could accomplish that. Another problem with that theory is some of those entrances are only safe at certain levels of the tide which adds another difficulty. My plan was to leave when my odds were best to get good weather. If and when bad weather hit us, we would ride it out away from the traffic and choppier waters near shore. My object was to get out past the continental shelf where the chop is less. There might be enormous waves but they are further apart and more comfortable as well as more maneuverable than the chop.

We hesitated leaving Neah Bay until the fog lifted to at least a quarter to a half mile of visibility but that turned out to be almost a joke. Once we were well out of the harbor the fog settled right back down; at that point the Canadian coast guard was extremely helpful. We had maintained a radio watch on the traffic control station and at the request of the Canadian Coast guard we reported our location at frequent intervals. They then reported the location of cargo ships close to us that we were unable to see in the fog. I had several radar reflectors up in the rigging but I wasn't confident that this little fiberglass craft would show up on their radar screens despite those reflectors. We felt really fortunate when most of those freighters made a left turn south very soon after exiting the Strait. When an Oil tanker was coming down from Alaska straight toward us the Canadian Coast Guard requested them to maintain direct radio contact with us until they had passed us. We never did see them due to the fog but did hear the throb of the engines; that was very spooky.

Suddenly, 60 miles out, the sun broke through. The fog lifted to display a very breathtaking sight: commercial fish boats all around us in every direction. How was it that we didn't collide, snag a line or have some other problem? I can't imagine the answer other than extremely good luck and maybe they were being wary of us but I have not found that to be the case in future instances.

Most people who experience seasickness do so the first hours and/or days at sea. Usually this dissipates at the end of three days. While I don't tend toward seasickness I do feel "off" the first two to three day. Brian and Joy however didn't follow that pattern. They were healthy the first few days.

By the time we were way out there heading south on a beam reach, the most efficient point and my favorite point of sail, the wind piped up to actual gale force at times. At one point in time we had reduced sail down to a double reefed main and a stay sail and for a brief time just a stay sail. Mighty Merry wasn't pounding into these huge waves, which we would have done had we been sailing closer to the wind. Rather she was skimming along at maximum speed until the point where one of those monstrous waves was ready to break and then would veer off just a bit, then hesitate as though taking a breath until the wave broke. We would ride along that crest instead of it crashing over us and then she would head back on course.

My favorite piece of equipment was the self steering wind vane which was doing all this for us. The wind steering vane is a contrast to the electronic steering vane. The mechanics of the instrument utilizes the wind to keep the boat on a consistent course relative to the wind. The electronic vane maintains a directional course to which it is set. I would only use it in very calm seas in tight circumstances if I needed to leave the tiller for some reason. Our safety depended on keeping the best course relative to the wind. It was up to me to plan that course.

How high were those waves? The closest I can come to a measurement is to point out that I had to crane my neck way back to lift my eyes high enough to see the top of it as it came toward us. While they were enormously high these waves were far apart so it wasn't a constant bashing. I soon learned to have confidence that this pattern of veering off and hesitating while the wave broke would continue and I learned to enjoy it but Joy and Brian became sea sick. While Joy recovered to some degree Brian never did and I have been forced to conclude that the fact he was not in charge, as he would have been on his own boat, added to the psychological effects that contributed to his seasickness.

The lesson I learned was three people were just too many for a trip of this sort on this small craft.

Seven full days later we arrived at 2:30 a.m. at the public marina in San Francisco, almost adjacent to the St. Francis Yacht Club. Of course the fog descended again as we neared San Francisco but never as dense as that stretch after Neah Bay.

The conclusion of that passage provided more relief than the conclusion of any other I can think of. I maintained it was because of the seasick crew but in retrospect there were other contributing factors which mostly involved my own psychology. It was my first experience of being that far from any port for that long a time and my first experience with near gale force winds creating gigantic waves while we had no alternative but to ride it all out. I could tell myself that I had experienced much of what there is to be afraid of out there on that big ocean and Mighty Merry Too proved she could handle it. I mostly enjoyed it so I could breathe a sigh of relief and tell myself that I hadn't bitten off more than I could chew.

Over the years since I have been asked hundreds of times, "Aren't you scared out on that big ocean?" I'll grant you I've had some uncomfortable moments but thinking about it and comparing it to driving on any major city thoroughfare I conclude city express way driving on a Friday evening is much more hazardous.

Very shortly after our arrival another small craft came in; a Japanese couple who had made a straight shot from Japan. It had been a very slow long trip for them and their waterline was covered with gooseneck barnacles. Somehow it seemed significant to learn that we each had started sailing in our youth on the same design little center board boat; a Snipe, and each had progressed next to a Star, an Olympic class racing boat. Life's little coincidences can lead to all kinds of mythological or theological conclusions.

It was with a real sense of accomplishment that I called my 93 year old mother to tell her of the trip but the wind was truly blown out of my sails when I heard her latest story. She lived on the top floor of a Florida condo on the Indian River and Intercostal Waterway and always expressed a great deal of interest in hearing about my adventures. My brother Walt lived in the same town and generally looked out for her but he was out of town for a much-needed vacation and therefore had arranged for someone to look in on her once a day.

The previous night she had wakened to see a burglar at the foot of her bed. She joked about the fact that when she sat up and told him to get out he must have thought she was a witch because he immediately did just that but she was very shaken, as any one of us would be. It did enter my thoughts that perhaps she had hallucinated but no, there was evidence he had been there.

It didn't take me long to arrange to fly to Florida as well as someone to look out for Mighty Merry Too in my absence. My brother arrived shortly after me so together we made new arrangements for her. While she was still mobile and alert she was very very frail. She frequently talked about the many changes she had seen during her lifetime. What leap from her own horse and buggy to high school to watching a number of space shots take off from nearby Cape Canaveral as well as, via television, watching the astronauts walk on the moon. Her last words upon my departure back to San Francisco and Mighty Merry were, "Don't you dare come back for a funeral. If you do, I'll haunt you!" It was the last time I would see her.

While I would eventually actually circumnavigate the world my plans at that time were no more definite than to sail to the Sea of Cortez in Mexico. I was only planning one step at a time which wasn't really a very practical approach since there were hurricane seasons to be considered, as well as the fact that it was often far easier to sail in one direction than another. Those who chose for instance to return to California from the Sea of Cortez either had a slow and tortuous beat back or took the long route and sailed all the way to Hawaii from Mexico and then back to the West Coast of the USA.

At each stop along the way I become acquainted with someone that I would spend time with again in some distant part of the world or, alternatively, would spend time with people from my past. My deceased brother's family was in California as well as the son of a close friend from Michigan so I stopped in most of the ports below San Francisco and was given a warm welcome in each instance. My entrance to Monterey is the one I remember most vividly because Mother Nature intervened to provide a dramatic few moments.

I had already made arrangements by radio for a slip at the city marina when a small dinghy came out to greet me to offer the use of a mooring at no charge to me. I not only would save money, but I would be more comfortable. I prefer a mooring to being tied up at the dock simply for the privacy it offers and the freer feeling of swinging with the tide and current. I had no more than grabbed hold of the mooring line and gotten attached when I felt a most peculiar jolt. Things inside the cabin were tossed around almost as though I were in a rough sea. It was quite disturbing so I immediately turned on the am/fm radio thinking I might learn something. It was silent. I tuned to one station after another to static and silence; it was many minutes before emergency messages began to be broadcast. That jolt was the result of an earthquake; a rather severe one in fact. I fared a lot better than most of the land people did but San Francisco fared even worse. Very recently I learned that strange jolt was the result of a mini tsunami coming across from Santa Cruz.

While San Diego was the jumping off spot for most people cruising to the Baja the harbor master at Monterey pointed out all the reasons why it was smarter to do my preparation in Monterey. I can honestly say that I have never been in any other American port where I was treated with as much special consideration, courtesy, friendliness, and honesty. I'm embarrassed to point out one example. Somehow I was careless enough to lose my billfold. The finder took it to the police station and the police made inquiries until somebody figured out the owner of that driver's license. Credit cards, cash, and all were intact.

Eventually I did continue on to San Diego which was a very slow trip with extremely light winds but very memorable. While eating dinner in the cockpit I watched the whales playing around me. I've experienced something like that now in three oceans and several seas but I am always equally charmed by these enormous creatures of the deep and they are one of many reasons I never considered anything but continuing with this life style.

Due to more family concerns I spent a number of months in San Diego so, since I still really didn't know if I was going to survive financially I used some of the time to put myself in a position to be able earn more money, if needed. I took some classes and then took the Coast Guard exams and earned a 100 Ton Captain's license. I was completely surprised by some of that; I had only applied for a 25-ton license but I was handed the 100-ton exam and passed it. Such a license was required for the skipper of any vessel carrying paying passengers.

I upgraded my ham license since I finally memorized Morse code well enough to pass the test. The truth is I've never used Morse code since, and haven't retained it in my memory; the license allowed me to use voice.

While a landlubber I had a teaching certificate and other credentials to keep me employable. Now I had credentials to keep me employable at sea.Most of the opportunities that readily came my way, and there were many, were proposals to deliver other peoples sailboats. Usually these were in some distant romantic location and the owner wanted the vessel back in the USA. The question I always asked was why didn't the owner want to sail it back? Because of the condition of the boat? While not always the answer it frequently was, although probably the most frequent reason was time. Someone still in mid career often used some vacation time to enjoy getting their boat to a destination but simply couldn't afford the time to get it back home. Although living on a shoe string, I managed to get by without actually utilizing that Captain's License.

One day I finally did set off for the Sea of Cortez and beyond. I really didn't know what to expect from the Baja except that it was such an attractive destination for so many people. I had spent some time during my youth at the University of Michoacan, in Morelia, Michoacan, Mexico, so I felt some affinity before even arriving. t one time I had a fair command of the language so I expected to be able to communicate which was more than most other cruisers I knew had going for them.

The biggest event during the sail down to the Baja was another visit by the United States Coast Guard. This time however they were utilizing a United States Navy Ship. Can you imagine how I felt as a huge destroyer approached this little craft and announced they were going to board me? The ordered me to maintain course and speed which was difficult if not impossible since they took away my wind and the ship itself provided a current. Further, I didn't appreciate the heavy black boots on deck and in my cockpit. They were courteous and I suppose most of my negative feelings about the event stem from the fact they offered and agreed to radio my exact position after getting back to the big ship but I never heard a word from them. A broken promise has a great influence on my opinion of anyone.

THE USS LYNNE D MCCORMICK

COAST GUARD BOARDING PARTY FROM NAVY SHIP

Once I arrived in Cabo San Lucas, where I first cleared customs, it became a very social time. While I had departed San Diego much later than the bulk of the many cruisers heading that direction, some of us were still filtering in. The biggest memory I have of Cabo is "Uncle Earl" on Ta De Me Ro. A large group of us were about to head in to shore to have dinner together in a local restaurant when two other small boats came in and dropped anchor; one of them considerably smaller than MM Too. Both appeared to be single handed. I was assigned the task of inviting them to join the crowd so I jumped in my dinghy to do just that. Jean Michelle, a young Frenchman readily assented but Earl, on the smaller boat, grumped "Do I gotta wear a suit? I have one but I only wear it on an airplane." The three of us ended up sitting at a table together so our conversation evolved into "what do you answer to the repetitive questions single-handlers are always asked?" The most common question is "what do you do at night?" Jean Michelle and I both answered and then Earl harrumphed and said, in strong Scandinavian accent, "oh that's crazy. I just drop all my sails and go down below and sleep."

It was quite apparent that we were each very far apart in age but I was startled when the young Frenchman asked "Maree, how old are you?" At the time I was a few weeks shy of 60 and so responded and then he pointed out that the three of us were each 30 years apart in age; at 30 years old he was the youngest, then me and then Earl, a few weeks shy of 90. That was in 1990 so I was thrilled to read in a magazine article that Earl, in 1996, was still out wandering the ocean alone. He was preparing to depart for the Marianas at that time.

While most of the year spent in Mexico was interesting and a pleasure one highly dramatic night stands out. I assume it was a mating ritual and I suspect it may be an annual or somewhat regular affair but I have never talked to anyone who knew more nor have I learned about it reading, talking to biologists or surfing the web. It was a time when the phosphorescence was very plentiful so when a circle of Manta rays came near the boat they really stood out. It was late afternoon when this began and was soon dark.

There was a great deal of phosphorescence in the water. A circle of rays appeared as a lighted whirling dervish when suddenly three of the rays leaped into the air in a pancake position apparently mating. When they rejoined the circle three more leaped into the air and so it went. The only change made was that the circle seemed to increase in velocity as well as in phosphorescence. Before long, another circle of rays appeared, and then another and another and countless more until I was watching an innumerable number of these glowing circles whirling in every direction around me while three leaped from each circle. The numbers of circles and intensity of their circling increased until the wee hours of the morning when they slowly began to dissipate although it was noon before they were all gone.

There was one more addition to this drama; in the wee hours of the morning a small pod of whales came in, circled around and through the harbor, under and around the various anchored boats as well as the whirling dervishes. They stayed until almost daylight and departed as a group. All of this was so vividly visible because of the enormous quantity of phosphorescence in the water. The occupant of one other vessel anchored nearby said that eleven years earlier he had been with his father in this same location at the same week of the year when a similar event had taken place. There were marine biologists on a research project at a nearby island and I finally sought them out for more information. The answer from them was, "Mary, I think you know more about this phenomenon than anyone we know of."

Mighty Merry Too spent hurricane season in this area before I finally sailed over to mainland Mexico visiting some of the popular tourist spots as well as lesser-known harbors. The Gulf War was declared the night I sailed across from Puerto Escondido to the mainland port of Mazatlan.

Jan, the friend who had spent time with me up in British Columbia, arrived to spend a month with me in Mexico. Due to a prior illness she had inner ear problems and had been taking a prescribed medication. Without telling me these facts she decided to stop taking the medication because it did tend to make her sleepy. We left to sail across the Sea of Cortez, a 2 — 3 day trip just as the Gulf War was declared. Our departure was under light winds, which slowly increased and moved from our beam to directly behind us; fast but not very comfortable as it always creates a roll. As the downwind roll developed Jan became seasick. I had a variety of seasick medications in my first aid kit including oral tablets or capsules, a patch that allowed the medication slowly into one's system and suppositories. I offered medication in the form of the patch as it was too late for oral tablets or capsules; they wouldn't remain in the body long enough to be absorbed. She refused. I offered the suppositories. She refused. I insisted she remain on the cabin sole (floor) as it was the center of gravity and would offer the most comfort but it also meant it was very difficult for me to move anywhere to get at navigation equipment, radios etc. There was always the possibility of accidentally stepping on her.

After she turned down the offers of suppositories I urged her to accept one. Finally things reached the point I began to worry about dehydration and felt strong steps needed to be taken. Just a few months previous I had observed dehydration become life threatening to another friend. I remembered she came from a naval family and held a great respect for the authority of the Captain of the ship. My Coast Guard license showing my authority as Master of up to 100-ton vessels was right over her head. It was time to quit being the sweet little gray haired lady. I pulled out the plastic box containing the suppositories, unwrapped one, handed it to her stating, "The Captain orders you to use this now or I will put it up your ass for you." She did. Within 20 minutes she was much improved. Within a few hours when we came in to our destination in pea soup fog her vision, much better than mine, was an enormous asset to us.

While in Mazatlan I shopped in Mexican supermarkets, frequently ate in restaurants frequented by upper-class Mexicans but almost never by tourists, and observed week after week that I saw no beggars on the street. Suddenly one day I saw beggars swarming down toward the waterfront and sure enough, in a matter of minutes a massive cruise ship came in, tied up at the wharf and disgorged hundreds of gringos long enough to shop at the tourist traps and donate to the beggars.

When I tied up at a dock, rather than anchored out in a harbor, it was usually at the docks built for the many resort condos cropping up in this part of the world. In one instance the dock master sent me over to the very newest dock where there wasn't another boat or sign of life. The condos were totally unoccupied since they probably weren't completed as yet. I had only been there for minutes before a security guard came by and greeted me in clear and articulate English. He offered me reassurance that I need not worry about being in such an isolated area because he would be sure that I remained unmolested.

I inquired where he had learned to speak such fluent English. "Why, picking pickles." This really prompted my curiosity because I had grown up in a small town where the largest Heinz pickle processing plant was located. My deceased brother had worked summers in his youth working for Heinz as manager of the Mexican work camps. Sure enough, he was talking about the same location.

I learned another thing about the many condos being built. None were ever totally completed for a very practical reason: a very large tax was imposed upon official completion.

It was time to think about what and where next: back up north or continue on south? South to where? Well, back up north meant beating against very light winds which is why so many people hired someone to bring their boat back. Why do that when I had no particular reason I needed to return? What were the alternatives if I went south? Nicaragua, Guatemala, Costa Rica and Panama. Well, the first two weren't greeting foreign cruisers with open arms but Costa Rica had a reputation for doing so. Then there was the clincher: no hurricanes. Hurricanes were then and still are the most fearsome events the ocean provides. Even a tsunami isn't much of a hazard to a boat at sea. As I made my decision I was very unaware of the many other benefits I would find in Costa Rica.

By now I had bonded with a number of couples, most of whom were planning to go through the Panama Canal and then head up the east coast of the USA. They would also be spending hurricane season in Costa Rica. They were planning to take the coastal route to avoid the Papagayo.

In many places around the world, a particular type of wind has a name. In California, Santa Ana winds blow hot out of the desert through Santa Ana Pass, drying the brush and then fanning the flames of wildfires. In the Adriatic Sea, they speak of the cold Bora from Hungary. The Rocky Mountains of the United States experience Chinook winds, abrupt warming breezes that follow a cold snap. The famous Mistral winds are cold, dry winds from the north that blow over the Mediterranean Sea and there are many more.

In the Central American winter there are Tehuanos and Papagayos. These are gale-force winds from the Gulf of Mexico and Caribbean Sea that funnel through narrow breaks in the Cordillera, gusting to wind speeds normally found only in major hurricanes. The Papagayo wind shrieks over the lakes of Nicaragua, a jet of wind that pushes far out over the Gulf of Papagayo on the Pacific coast.

As I read some of the guide books and listened to some of the "experts" I realized this was beginning to sound like the debate of how to sail from Seattle to California. The theory I read was to sail "one foot on the beach" to avoid the devastation of the Papagayos.

This was just fine for those with two or more people but just wasn't something a single handed sailor could accomplish safely so, once more I studied just how far out into the Pacific did I have to go to get beyond the Papagayos? 400 miles was the best answer I could come up with. in that case I might as well head for Cocos Island, which, after a little study, sounded very attractive.

What attracted me to Cocos Island? It is a 24 sq. kilometer typical tropical island with two bays in the north, Wafer Bay and Chatham

Bay, which are divided by a ridge. Chatham Bay is the better anchorage of the two but there are times when neither is very safe. Finding enough sand bottom is the primary problem. The rest of the coastline is very steep with quite a number of waterfalls, some of them 200 feet high. The highest point, called mount "Iglesias", is almost 3000 feet high. The climate is hot and humid — very very humid. Between March and December it rains for a couple of hours almost every day. There are many romantic tales stating that the richest treasure in the world is buried on Cocos Island. At least one person spent 25 years searching for it. The pirate named Benito Bonito, who sailed the "Relampagao" and raided every city along the Pacific coastline is said to have buried treasure there. Captain Thompson was supposed to have brought the wealth of Lima on the "Mary Dear" in 1821. Is it the Treasure Island of Robert Louis Stevenson's "Treasure Island?" That is probably what attracted me the most and I could after all avoid the hazards of sailing "one foot on the beach", as well as the dreaded Papagayo by taking that route. So why not?

While mulling these thoughts over, I received a radio call from Mark on Quicksilver, a craft a bit larger than mine, manned by a young single handed sailor I had met way back in Half Moon Bay, California. Mark had set out, accompanied by a girlfriend, a year or more after I had left. Now he was headed for Costa Rica where he had employment waiting for him with a group who took tourists on Kayaking trips. The girlfriend had decided this wasn't the life for her so now Mark also was single-handed; wouldn't it be a good idea if we were to buddy boat? Well —.maybe but probably not. Still I'm a pretty sociable type and he offered some valid arguments. I had communication with the rest of the world via my ham radio, which he found desirable. By then I also had a GPS, which was still a pretty new technology, and in my lexicon very expensive. He had radar which I certainly would love to have had back up in the fog of the Pacific Northwest. I also had more offshore experience by then, but I've never figured out how that would help someone in another boat.

Regardless of my remaining slight misgivings we did set off from Zihuatanejo together along with an accompanying whale. Yes, that is the truth. I set off a little ahead of Quicksilver and was accompanied by a fairly small whale for an hour or more. If I were of a superstitious nature and I added up all my whale visitations I would say the gods were sending the whales to protect me or, more likely, to keep enticing me forward in my journeys.

The winds were little more than a gentle breeze but enough to keep us slowly moving toward Cocos Island. Still, they were so gentle that on a couple evenings we shared dinner. Quicksilver came alongside, rafted off from Mighty Merry and we shared a vegetable quiche that he had made or some fresh bread I had baked and so on it went. Our first goal was to get far enough off shore to be safe from the Papagayo. We weren't in a well-traveled area so we weren't getting the frequent weather predictions so often available via the VHF or ham radio although I was in touch with other hams and had a regular evening conversation with friends in various parts of the world from Alaska to Panama.

The local (Mexican and Central American) fish boats weren't always too conscientious in keeping with VHF regulations and etiquette so there were frequent bursts of chatter in Spanish of which I could understand bits and pieces. This provided proof that we were not entirely alone out here since VHF transmission travels a relatively short distance except in very rare instances when strange atmospheric phenomena carries it via a skip to vast distances. One night we heard a lot of such chatter and also saw the lights of the vessel coming directly at us. We made an effort at communication with no response and suddenly Mark, Quicksilver's skipper, was convinced these were pirates. At his insistence I followed his lead in turning off all lights and he tracked them on his radar. Once our lights were out they diverted and eventually disappeared. I have always believed they were simply curious fishermen but regardless I don't care to meet strangers in the middle of the night in a rarely traveled part of the ocean. In the unlikely event they had evil intentions in mind I was relieved they weren't as well equipped as our combined resources since they evidently didn't have radar to track us.

In the meantime the winds became lighter and lighter and it became very clear that we were in the doldrums. I had anticipated a very slow trip but Quicksilver began to fret. If he were already in Costa Rica maybe Jim's girlfriend would be trying to communicate with him to patch up their quarrel and after all he was obligated to get there by a not too distant date to begin his employment. At this rate he wouldn't have any time to spend at Cocos after he arrived.

When it was clear we were far enough past the danger of a Papagayo and there was a choice to either continue to Cocos or head straight for mainland Costa Rica he tried to convince me to head straight for Costa Rica. Then he determined that he would motor; another choice I was unwilling to make out of preference as well as the fact that I didn't carry enough diesel to do so even if I wanted to. He mulled this over and calculated that he had sufficient fuel to motor if he diverted straight to the mainland but he too would run short if he tried to get to Cocos first. Since his impatience wouldn't allow him not to motor the choice was obvious and we said "bon voyage" to each other.

Later, the same day when Quicksilver had been out of sight but a short time I suddenly saw in the distance behind me a very large mast, overtaking me quite rapidly. The size of the approaching hull continued to surprise me but the puzzle was rather quickly solved via the VHF when Suvetar, a 75 foot vessel hailed the Mighty Merry. It was a large vessel, with a sizeable crew and the many luxuries a 24-foot vessel rarely has: refrigeration being the most notable. I was probably moving less than one knot so I happily dropped sail and accepted the offer of a dinghy ride to Suvetar's deck to enjoy a cold drink and the offer of fresh fruit and veggies to carry back to Mighty Merry Too. They offered diesel as well, in the event I was short, but since my engine had barely been used since I last filled my tank I suggested they use their engine to catch up to Quick Silver and make the diesel offer to him which he was almost certain to accept. They were heading straight to Costa Rica anyway and I continued pleasantly on.

I was only a few days away from the island when I had another new experience; this one was a bit scary. A number of very black clouds began moving into the area and suddenly I saw a waterspout coming down out of one of the clouds. I had never seen one before but it looked exactly like a miniature of the pictures I had seen of tornados which is exactly what it is. Knowing it could contain some tremendous winds I prepared to change course but then I saw another waterspout in the direction I preferred. Okay, turn the other way then. Whoops, there was a third water spout. I was fascinated since it was a completely new experience but I admit to a few moments of fear as well. I was quite relieved when all three headed far enough away from me that I could enjoy just observing.

I was also one of the last boats allowed to visit Cocos Island in this casual manner. It is a Costa Rican National Park and today is preserved, as a true nature reserve and one must obtain a permit well in advance. Nobody lives on the island and no camping is allowed. There were two park rangers who greeted me and asked to see my passport saying they thought they were supposed to collect some fees but they didn't know how much so forget it. Additionally they would welcome some petrol for their outboard if I had any extra, which I really didn't.

Several French boats were present as well as more single handed craft than almost anywhere I have ever visited. The skipper of the larger of the French boats met me by dinghy to point out the difficulty of finding a spot with sufficient sand in which to dig in an anchor. While I spent a long time in the search for a sandy bottom, I probably located one of the very best spots in the anchorage. The proof came during one of the big blows we experienced when I was the only boat not to drag anchor. While patience isn't one of my strong virtues I have tended to be very patient when searching for a suitable anchorage. She was my home after all.

Jean Pierre, the other Frenchman, and one of the single handled sailors present was my closest neighbor on a very modern craft with a stern platform at water level. He stood on that platform almost every day to fish and very frequently shouted over, "Maree, would you like a feesh for dinner?" and I most happily accepted the offer. One day as he stood right there at water level a shark leaped out of the water to grab the fish on his hook. I screamed in terror but he laughed although I noted thereafter he fished from the cockpit.

The six weeks I spent at Cocos actually became very social and presented me with some curious experiences. Two other American boats were present, both with couples I had spent time with in Mexico: Glenn and Kathleen on Wings ,and Grace and Einar on Egret. Several American boats came in for only a few days, as they were eager to continue on to the South Pacific. One I remember so distinctly because of its unusual characteristics and unusual crew: four retired engineers and the wife of one of them. The boat was designed by an Italian, built in Spain and had an enormous amount of equipment in duplicate including Volvo engines, which I considered notorious for their frequent failures. (One person I knew bought a Volvo engine for his boat only to discover it was out of warranty before he purchased it.) Additionally, most of the multitude of other electronics was not working. My thought was "where else is there so much equipment that doesn't work in the hands of so many engineers?" I did hear from them several years later; they had completed a circumnavigation which was proof enough for me that they did eventually figure it all out.

Additionally, two commercial dive boats came in almost weekly. One, an Israeli owned vessel, came in from the Mainland with divers from a variety of countries but mostly American. They would stay about five to seven days. About the time they left a Costa Rican (American owned I think) boat came in with a load of divers. Cocos is one of the premier dive sites of the world and both boats were booked at least two years in advance. The main attraction wasn't coral but sharks. At one of the small islands adjacent to Cocos there are a large number of hammerhead sharks, a major attractions to the divers but the hammerheads spent their time in waters far too deep for me.

The very clear water was a delight for snorkeling, which a group of us did at least twice a day. In the morning we went lobster hunting. I wasn't very efficient with the spear so I accepted the task of taking the speared lobster back to the dinghy while Einar and Grace from

Egret and Glen and Kathleen from Wings did the actual searching and spearing. There were always lots of sharks in the area so the trick was to swim back to the dinghy with the speared lobster well up out of the water. As long as there wasn't blood or an open wound in the water the sharks left us completely alone until late afternoon when they became aggressive. For this reason we were always out of the water by 4:00 p.m. I was very skittish in the beginning but became accustomed to having sharks around me while snorkeling but I never gained the courage to do as Einar did. He actually chased a shark into what he thought was its home hole.

A VERY TASTY LUNCH FROM THE LAST SWIM

The dive boats became the resource that allowed me to remain at the island for the many weeks that I did while still maintaining a reasonable diet of fresh foods to supplement all the lobster and fish I consumed. They both came with huge supplies of fruit and vegetables intended for the paying guests. They commonly had a large supply remaining when preparing to depart and for some reason offered them all to me. Invariably it was more than I could use or store so I then took a good part of the treasure trove around by dinghy to the other sailboats for them to share. One of the dive boats also sent their dinghy out to fish every morning at the crack of dawn in order to supply their guests. I frequently heard the motor of the dinghy up close and when I looked out an enormous fish (usually Mahi Mahi) was being placed in my dinghy. When I say huge it means the head was hanging over one end and the tail over the other end; hanging so far over that I tried to care for it promptly so it didn't become a shark's dinner.

That contribution usually led to a festive evening. I immediately took the fish to the large French boat because they 1) had refrigeration and 2) the skipper, Jacques, was very adept at cleaning and preparing the fish for the evening barbecue and their cockpit was large enough for all of us to be seated. My next task was to make the rounds of the anchorage and invite the residents for a potluck. The guests were expected to bring their own plates and cutlery as well as a dish to share.

Jean Pierre invariably brought a few bottles of quite good wine. His parents had a vineyard back home. I marveled at the lovely crystal wine glasses Jacques and Marie provided and finally at one of these festive events inquired how they dared to carry such fragile items on board a sailboat. "Ah Maree, when the Germans took over my family's farm my parents quickly buried whatever they could and then had a huge bonfire over the buried items. After the war when they returned to the farm they dug down and found the family crystal. We think if they could survive the Nazis they can survive what the ocean has to offer."

Cocos is a jungle covered mountainous island which is part of its beauty. There are many waterfalls and almost no trails. The waterfalls provided us with plenty of fresh drinking water. One of the dive boats had rigged a huge hose from one of the falls, which was accessible from the beach so it was easy to fill jerry jugs and take them home by dinghy. Additionally a nearby waterfall was a perfect "Laundromat" as you can see..

One day someone announced; "it's time for a hike." The largest waterfall was far up the side of the mountain. The infrequently used trail, mostly overgrown, but findable led to the fresh water lake below the falls. In that tropical heat walking that trail was a huge expenditure of effort but there was a lovely cool fresh water swim awaiting us when we finally arrived.

A few weeks later another hike was announced. I learned the destination and quickly turned chicken since such effort in this tropical heat was beyond my constitution. During World War II an American military aircraft had crashed on one of the mountain peaks and a number of people were very curious to see the remains. It didn't sound like my kind of venture under any circumstances but I was very distressed when I heard the end results. The Park Rangers had insisted that if a group were going they must accompany them; to which there were no objections. It was believed that it had been many years since any group had gone up there so the trip would be considerably harder than the one I had found very difficult.

When the group reached the site they found, in the wrecked plane, a watch with an inscription. It had obviously belonged to one of the airmen. The hikers wanted to get it to the US authorities with the hopes of ultimately getting it to the family of the deceased. The Park Rangers insisted it was their duty to turn it over to the Costa Rican government to request that they return it to the US authorities; this seemed appropriate. The trouble with that argument is that a few days later they accidentally dropped it in the water and lost it. If you surmise that I didn't think much of those Park Rangers you are correct.

One week when we were expecting the Costa Rican dive boat a much larger ship came in its place. On board was a goodly percentage of the Costa Rican elected government officials as well as the usual scuba dive aficionados and dive guides from the previous smaller boat. In addition to the diver's guides was a young Costa Rican biologist, Maria. This vessel was normally used to take large groups of tourists to some of the coastal national parks and Maria acted as their guide. One of the primary interests for tourists is the multitudes of colorful and exotic birds in the Costa Rican parks. The owner of the ship had aspirations of building a hotel on Cocos Island. He had brought these lawmakers to visit with the hopes he could convince them to grant permission for such a venture. I am pleased to say that part of their trip was a failure.

I was fascinated with all Maria was able to tell me about the local flora and fauna and she introduced me to a number of the guests on board including Mauricio and Jose and their elderly mother. Mauricio and Jose were part of a large and politically powerful family. The woman they called mother was actually the woman who had been their nursemaid as children. Their mother died when they were still very young and they truly thought of her as their mother. She was fascinated with my boat and my travels and Maria conveyed the message to me of how she dreamed of being able to sail on Mighty Merry.

She was old, not very agile, and didn't speak English, although I did speak enough Spanish to communicate with her. To invite her for a sail was very tempting but it did seem there were a lot of obstacles to be overcome due to her lack of agility. Maria offered to accompany us if I took her. The ship's crew offered to help her getting from the big vessel to my little craft while the weather was almost ideal with steady but gentle breezes from a direction that meant I could take her some distance at the most comfortable point of sail, and could return at the same point of sail, simply on the other side. You know the answer of course and I have never been so rewarded for such a pleasant task as it turned out to be. I shall never forget the pleasure I saw in her eyes as we sailed some distance around the island and back. That would have been all the thanks anyone would have needed but Mauricio and Jose made sure I had their phone numbers and made it clear they expected me to call when I came to the mainland. The result of all that was visits to their homes, hotel rooms gratis (they owned the oldest continuously operating hotel in San Jose and later built more large hotels) and the knowledge that whenever I needed information or assistance they were available. Most important of such contacts is the opportunity to see the country from the view of the residents rather than the tourist view. So when I finally departed Cocos Island for mainland Costa Rica I found a warm reception and stayed a full six months before departing for points beyond.

Chatham Bay holds a unique guest book hundreds of inscriptions chiseled in boulders along the tiny bay. The oldest are from the late 18th century like "His.Brit.Maj. Schr. LES DEUX AMIS - 1797", followed by dozens of others throughout the 19th century and from the treasure hunters of the 20th century. One of the more recent was from Jacques Cousteau. The one for Mighty Merry Too is so poorly carved that I admit it is almost illegible. Carving in hard rock with inadequate tools in that hot humid atmosphere was extremely exhausting and I didn't have the servants those old ship had nor even the paid crew as Jacques Cousteau had.

After six weeks of such pleasure I finally departed for the mainland; a pleasant and uneventful sail except for the boobies. These large sea birds decided they liked the bow of Mighty Merry Too. The gentle winds that carried me along weren't strong enough to deter them and I was becoming weary of all the bird shit all over the bow but when I went forward with a pole to try to scatter them they began to attack me so I put up with them for many days until I finally encountered a squall. That squall not only cleaned off their shit but the boobies themselves much to my relief. While I'm an avid bird watcher on land, I've never learned to like boobies.

When I cleared customs upon entering at Punta Arenas I was given evidence that I was wise when I had chosen a route that kept me away from the Papagayos. The customs office was above a flight of very very narrow stairs where, on the way up, I encountered an Australian who engaged me in conversation despite the narrow quarters. He evidently was very hungry to have a conversation with someone who spoke English as my "excuse me" as I bumped him on the way up was enough to get him started into a long monologue. It was a hot and uncomfortable place to linger so I finally convinced him that as soon as I completed my business upstairs, (he was on his way down) I would meet him down below and let's go have a coffee or beer. It turns out he had sailed all the way from Australia single handed with no difficulty until meeting the Papagayo which had all but destroyed his boat. He had limped into harbor and while he considered it unrepairable, it didn't deter him from his planned single handed circumnavigation. He replaced the boat while in Costa Rica and I heard more about him much later when he lost another boat before he finally got back to Australia; but eventually he did make it. When people ask me if I'm not frightened out there in that big ocean I don't think of him or I would be.

Shortly after arriving in Costa Rica, prior even to clearing customs, I received a message via the ham radio that mother had died. I received that message within ten minutes of the time my brother had called my ham friend to pass that news on and I was warned once more that she had not wanted me to interrupt my journeys for a funeral. Minutes beforehand I had turned down an invitation to join a group for drinks and a dinner on shore. I changed my mind and joined the group long enough to offer a toast to my mother to whom I owe so much.

Cost Rica is a hurricane free part of the world so Mighty Merry was safe for the season while I had time to take advantage of so much opportunity for seeing new flora and fauna. 27% of the country is National Park or protected area ranging from cloud forest to active volcanoes. Earthquakes were so common that the intensity of yesterday's quakes were reported daily in the newspaper along with the weather. I didn't get many pictures of those parks since I accidentally dropped my camera into one of the many hot springs.

Costa Rica provided a rich variety of experiences including learning how to be just a little more careful when traveling alone. San Jose, the capitol and major city, is inland so I frequently took the bus to visit the many acquaintances I had made at Cocos and to arrange for tours etc. San Jose is a big city and has its share of poverty. While violent crimes like murder or rape are almost unheard of thievery is common. Like so many tropical countries, most of the people do take a siesta mid-day so on one trip to the city when my bus arrived at the usual destination at mid-day the streets were particularly empty. I knew the route from the bus station to my ultimate destination and had walked it many times so I proceeded to do the usual instead of taking one of the many very inexpensive little red taxis. I should have at least asked myself why nobody else walked or why there was nobody else on the street. A few blocks away from the bus station I suddenly felt someone trying to grab my fanny pack in which I carried my money and passport. A moment later the thief and I were down on the ground wrestling while I screamed, "mi passaporte no, no!!" I was already in the habit of carrying the pocket part of it in front rather than across my "fanny" as it was designed and evidently it wasn't easy for him to get the buckle unbuckled because I still had it on me when we were suddenly surrounded by little red taxis and he took off on foot.I hopped into the closest of the taxis. I was filthy from having rolled around on the ground wrestling but my possessions were all intact, I was uninjured, and had learned another lesson. Yes, I was more careful in the future although when telling the story of this event while in New Zealand I was startled at the strange looks on people's faces and finally the bursts of laughter. Finally I was told the word "fanny" had a very different meaning in New Zealand and I no longer referred to my pack as a "fanny pack".

As I mentioned there is poverty but despite that fact the literacy rate is 96%, one of the highest in the world. It was not uncommon to see a bag lady sitting on the curb reading a newspaper pulled from the trash.

As Christmas neared I was enchanted by the enormous Christmas tree in the major shopping mall. It seemed so different from ours and it took me a few minutes to grasp what I was reacting to. It was huge, live, placed in the middle of a central mall that was open to the ceiling of this multistoried mall. There were no commercial ornaments or lights but hundreds of hand made carvings and hand drawn pictures and blown glass. There was no effort to keep people away from touching it or touching the decorations and I saw no destructiveness on the part of those who did; young or old.

Gift giving was part of the tradition but expectations were different: one gift for a child. The rich might give their child a very expensive gift but a child only expected and usually received only one gift as well as some of the many treats provided such as candy, nuts and the most treasured: an apple from the USA. Apples were so treasured that there was a major effort to develop an apple tree that would thrive in that tropical environment.

While in Costa Rica I wanted to see more of the country, especially the national parks. Maria introduced me to a woman who acted as a guide for me and another couple. Spanish was her native language and she also spoke fluent German as her husband is German, but she spoke little English. This was satisfactory for us because the other couple, Grace and Einar from Egret had just completed an intensive language school and welcomed the practice. While they were taking the class the school arranged for them to live with a local family who spoke no English. By now I had regained enough fluency that I was comfortable with the arrangement. Our guide wasn't the biologist that Maria was but she was knowledgeable. More important was the fact she was very well acquainted with the rangers at the parks who served as excellent guides. We rented a car and she made all the arrangements for our overnight stays selected restaurants as well as planning the itinerary. The idea was to travel at the rate a local Costa Rican would pay while on holiday in contrast to an American tourist. The plan was very successful. Additionally we improved our Spanish language skills.

Speaking of language skills, I was quite surprised one evening at a large dinner party, when in mid conversation one of the Costa Ricans spoke up and said, "for goodness sakes let's speak English. It's so much easier. You have to use so many words to say the same thing in Spanish."

REFERENCE MAPS FOR FOLLOWING CHAPTERS

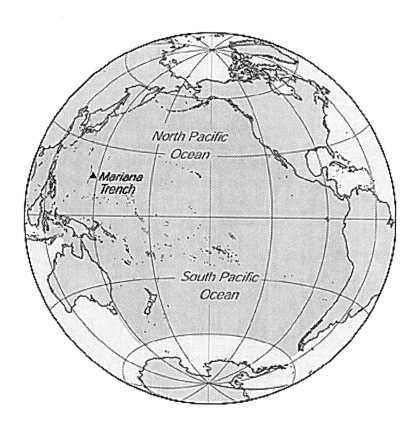

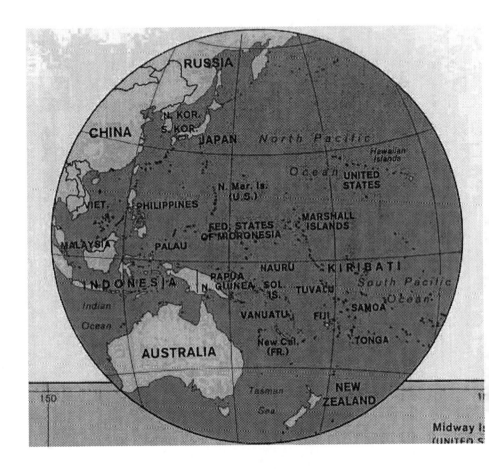

FRENCH POLYNESIA

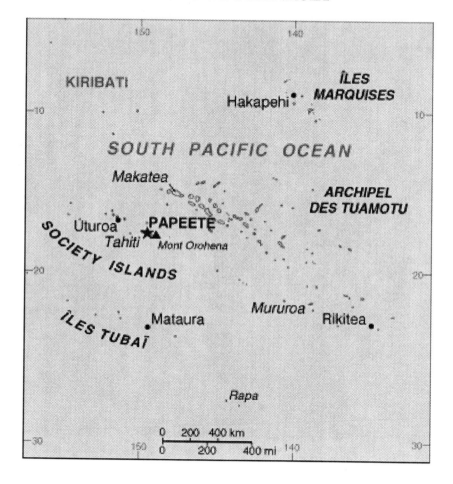

COOK ISLANDS

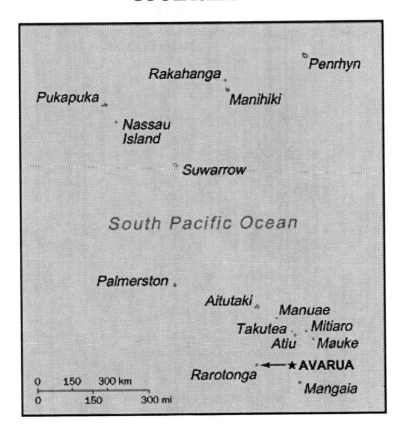

TONGA

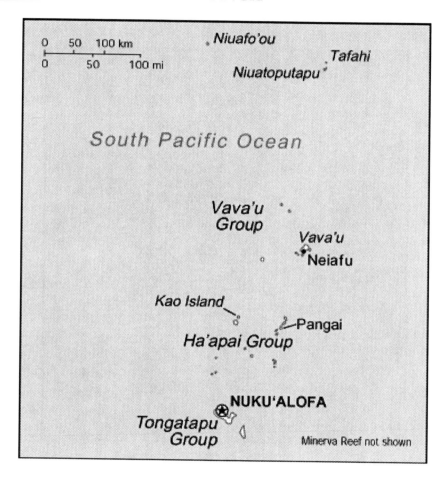

FIJI

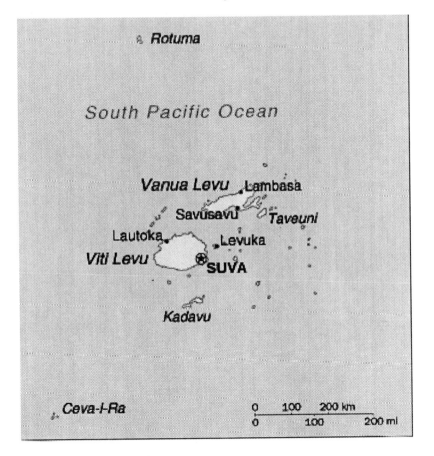

NEW ZEALAND

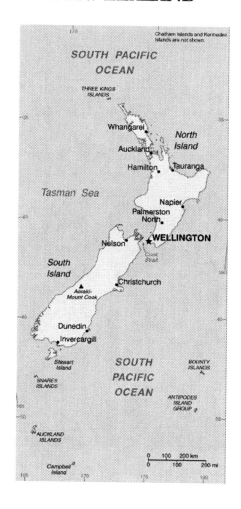

CHAPTER FIVE
ACROSS THE EQUATOR AND BEYOND

Late December, very shortly before Christmas, I departed on Mighty Merry Too for Ecuador, with a plan to go to the Galapagos Islands before heading for French Polynesia. Yes, I had decided after the long slow trip to Cocos that I could tolerate a long time at sea. No, I didn't have a visa permitting me to go to Galapagos. I hadn't even made an attempt to obtain a permit after talking to so very many people who had made the effort to do everything by the book. The process was convoluted, time consuming and in most instances resulted in having spent not only the time but also a lot of dollars with either negative results or no results. The latter was the most frustrating.

Eventually I began to understand the thinking process behind it all. Setting aside the corruption, of which there was plenty, the government recognized that there was profit for the government as, well as the hotels and guides in the islands, when large groups of people arrive on tour boats or by air. The cruising sailors offered little profit so were thought of as a nuisance; either they should be charged outrageous fees to discourage them or offer delay after delay until the applicant gives up in discouragement. In reality those that ignored the whole process and simply arrived were usually given a reasonable length of time to visit, depending on the port captain of the moment. So much for trying to be a good world citizen.

There was a bon voyage dinner the night before departure and I couldn't even get away at the crack of dawn without a crowd wishing me well. They had figured out my habits by now and managed to all get up early to wish me well as I set out to cross the Equator and beyond.

I was still in the doldrums so it was a very slow trip and I really hadn't yet learned to take advantage of the many squalls that came through which, today, seems the most sensible way to get through the doldrums. I tried to dodge the squalls or at least minimize sail. The braver or more knowledgeable single hander often treated those squalls as a benefit and kept their heading rather than dodging as well as maintaining enough sail to utilize the ferocious winds so often a part of the squall. My biggest concern was the traffic to the Panama Canal so I was particularly alert to both radios; my VHF and my long distance ham/ssb. I didn't think of time as an issue but I had told myself that my Christmas present would be to cross the Equator by Christmas day. I did make it by New Year's Day.

I was making such minimal progress that I finally resorted to using the engine far more than usual which also meant using the electronic auto pilot instead of my wind vane. Whoops, the autopilot promptly broke down. Hmmmm, what to do? Well, there would be little likelihood of getting it repaired when I did get to Ecuador so what could I lose by taking it apart to see if I could figure out what was wrong? I don't claim any electronic expertise here but I did take it apart, cleaned all the parts thoroughly, sprayed on some of my favorite lubricant (Boeshield) and simply put it back together and held my breath. *It worked.*I wasn't quite so lucky when I discovered I wasn't getting out on the ham radio. After a thorough inspection I saw that the antennae cable was frayed and almost completely disconnected. For several days I was able to hear but couldn't get my transmission out but eventually I could no longer hear either. Right then it seemed more important to me that I could use the VHF radio since this would be my communication to any vessels within view and/or within about 25 miles. I was crossing the path to the Panama Canal after all so I did want to hear any of that traffic.

The day before Christmas I did hear several fish boats and soon I was hailed by a very large fish boat wishing me a Merry Christmas.

Hearing and understanding on the radio is always a little more difficult than in conversation with a person in view, and since Spanish isn't my native language I always find it much more difficult to understand over the radio, but they were very clear. After we chatted for a few minutes they determined they wanted to give me a Tuna as a Christmas gift. It was a nice idea but really a joke. Bringing that huge vessel alongside my wee little craft did nothing but frighten me so I inquired if they had weather fax, being pretty sure they did. A weather prediction would be a lovely gift. They eagerly gave a positive response and would run one and relay the information. Not good news. No wind this side of the Galapagos, which was well to my west. I thanked them and they continued on and were soon out of sight. Within 20 minutes of their departure a lovely breeze came up and I was soon making good progress to my destination of Punta Arenas, Ecuador. So much for weather reports.

New Years Day, as I was approaching my destination, I heard two ships talking to each other on the VHF and one of them was most definitely an American voice. While I didn't see either ship I hailed them and the American responded. We chatted for a bit and he offered to call anyone I wanted to get messages to so I thought how much fun it would be to say "Happy New Year from the Southern Hemisphere", to my elder son who was in the military at the time. I knew from there he would relay to the rest of the family.

I had realized that there might be some people concerned about me because I hadn't been on the ham nets with the regularity that was usual for me. Single handed sailors were always given priority but my femininity gave me an extra measure of priority so I was almost invariably number one when checking into the net. I suppose I don't really have any idea of how many people were aware of my travels because there are countless numbers of hams that just listen in on many of these nets. Almost fifteen years later I am just becoming aware of this as occasionally I still receive a message from someone telling me I am their hero or some such.

MY NEW YEAR'S DESTINATION

I wasn't thinking of who was worrying about me while I was bubbling over with the enthusiasm of finally being south of the Equator and wanting to share that excitement with loved ones. I was suddenly numb with the shock that the United States Coast Guard and United States Navy were supposedly combing the waters between Costa Rica and Ecuador for this wee little craft just because I hadn't been up on the radio for a few days.

How and why would they even be aware of me? Oh. Someone on the ham net figured out how to call my son who at that time was a naval officer. (Easy to do since they often relayed phone calls to him for me.) Well, the truth is that he believes they were all out looking for me but what I believe is that an alert was sent out, "if you should see this little sailboat etc." I don't for one minute believe they sent out a bunch of ships looking for me, at least for the tax payers sake I hope not.

Later that same day I arrived in Salinas a beach town with a quite sumptuous yacht club, a few high rise condominiums, (today large numbers of them) and equally sumptuous homes built in the Latin American/Spanish style i.e. completely walled in. Most of these are vacation homes for the wealthy in Guayaquiel which is the largest city in the country. There was already an American boat, Watermelon with Jean and Peter, and a South African boat Obsession with Gary and Ingrid, at anchor off the beach. The skippers of these two boats came out to greet me as I circled around surveying the area. They had heard me on the ham radio for many months so were familiar with me while I hadn't the slightest idea who they were but they soon became fast friends and we are still in touch. Almost before I had time to get the hook down they delivered a new antenna cable to my cockpit and very soon installed it while they gave the information needed regarding clearing customs, bus connections to where this was done as well as provision shopping etc. etc.

Through a friend who once upon a time had been the American ambassador to Ecuador I had introductions to a family in Guayaquiel; Carlos and Rosanna Tama, so this huge and quite unpleasant city became part of the itinerary also. The Tama's had an apartment in one of the high rises here in Salinas as well but were rarely here. They insisted I take my laundry to their maid at the apartment "because she doesn't have anything to do most of the time anyway." When I think of the sumptuous homes and the beach high rise condos I remain surprised that there was no running water to any of these buildings. All were dependent on water trucks bringing in regular supplies to their personal storage tanks.

When I needed to exchange dollars for the local sucres the Tama's chauffeur took me to the park across from the bank and explained that I would get a much better exchange rate on the street than I would at the bank. Therefore he made the actual exchange for me. I would not have had the courage to do it.

Guayaquiel is really a very unpleasant city. Much of my memory of the unpleasantness is related to the strike of garbage workers that was taking place at the time, as well as a shortage of electricity due to a drought. The streets were piled high with plastic bags of garbage that had been accumulating for weeks. The Tama's home was in a lovely area of town but the commercial area is most unpleasant; dirty, crime filled and whenever I was there also hot and dark. The country had suffered a drought. The only power plant was at the site of a damn on a river coming down from the mountains. During the drought that plant could only produce a small fraction of the usual so electricity was being rationed; this was a perfectly reasonable thing to do if well planned and/or organized. It was anything but well organized. Here are some examples: certain businesses were scheduled to have power between 8 to noon every other day so the employees were told to come to work only at those times. More likely than not, what actually happened was chaos since the times the power came on bore little relationship to the schedule. The Tamas were especially frustrated. For years they had generated their own electricity for their soda pop producing plant; the source of their income. When the damn had been built they were required to buy their electricity from the government and forbidden to generate their own. Now there was little electricity to buy.

My best and worst memory of Ecuador is the guided tour I took, arranged by a travel agency in Guayaquiel. I was well aware that in Central and South America bus travel is usually preferable to trains. In fact there is a saying, "trains are for poor people." The problem with that is that the terrain I wanted to see between Guayaquiel and Quito was best seen by train because there are almost no roads since it goes straight up over some very rugged mountains. The travel agent pointed out that there was a special car for tourists that would provide first class travel including a dining section with a first class meal. I purchased a ticket at first class prices which included the company of an English speaking guide. I found it interesting that the accent of spoken Spanish differed significantly between each Latin country I visited as did the idioms so his English was helpful to me. I just didn't understand Ecuadorians as well as Mexicans or Costa Ricans.

In the hotel Guayaquiel, where I was staying, the door man advised me to not leave the building after dark except by taxi due to the prevalence of street crime. The police carried guns which were rarely loaded since they were required to pay for their own ammunition. They rarely were willing or able to do this. All first class restaurants had private well armed guards. The guide met me at the hotel in Guayaquiel and took me to the train station which was a good distance from the central city.

The train arrived approximately an hour late which by now was not a surprise to me, but what was a sickening surprise was that there was no first class car; it was out for repairs since there hadn't been sufficient reservations. Carlos, my guide, pointed out that the only sensible choice was to ride on the roof. On the roof? "Yes, at least there you can breathe fresh air and see all the scenery which is why you are making the trip in the first place. Look at the interior of the cars."

I did look inside and quickly recognized his point. There were as many animals, such as goats and chickens etc., as humans in the cars and they were all packed in like the proverbial can of sardines. Looking back I just can't imagine why I didn't just say "no way, I'm getting my money back." Instead I climbed the ladder to the roof and we sat down as the train began to chug forward. Once underway there was no alternative because the country we were going through had almost no continuous roads which were the reason for taking the train. We were going through the Andes Mountains after all. The roof was metal so that hot tropical sun soon turned it into a frying pan. After several hours we were climbing mountains or trying to climb them. It became obvious that engine just couldn't make it as it slowed and slowed and finally just stopped.

Not to worry, another engine was coming to assist. At least during the wait for the engine we were able to get off and walk around and cool down just a bit. The second engine helped for quite some distance when finally it too slowed and slowed some more and finally stopped. Therefore they would send a coal fired engine which had much more power than did these diesel engines. Well it did have more power but now we had the black smoke from the coal fired engine coming straight at us as well as the heat from the sun fired roof. By the time we reached our destination I was covered with black soot from head to toe and was physically sick.

It was an all day trip; we hadn't brought any food because there was going to be a first class diner so I became ravenous as well as miserably uncomfortable. Many of the other roof occupants were bringing farm produce to market in Quito, most of it fruit, and they were very generous in offering all we wanted but unwashed fruit didn't provide any benefit to my digestive system. The result of it all was I spent two full days unable to leave my hotel room in Quito. That was the disaster part of the trip.

NOT A COMFORTABLE WAY TO RIDE

BUT THIS WAS EVEN WORSE

From Quito I continued my tourist trip by air to the Galapagos which was a much more satisfactory visit. I had an added benefit of an introduction to the port captain who reassured me I would be very welcome were I to sail in on Mighty Merry Too. In the back of my mind when I left Costa Rica was the possibility of sailing to Chile. Through the friend of one of my guests I would have introductions to many people in Chile. Additionally I had been in regular radio contact with a Canadian sailor who had started out from British Columbia. I asked him how the Fjords of Chile compared to British Columbia. His answer was that they were very much the same as 100 years ago in BC. As attractive as that was to me I also kept hearing about the many pirate vessels out of the southern part of Peru and received a great many admonitions that discouraged me of the idea. Now that the Port Captain was encouraging I disabused myself of the idea of mainland Chile and decided instead on Galapagos and then on to Easter Island (which today is Chilean), Pitcairn and on to French Polynesia. I had proven to myself that I was capable and prepared for long distance crossings. So why not?

I departed Ecuador, planning to visit Galapagos again, but the first two weeks of the voyage were a real trial of my willingness to meet adversity. There were difficulties with my genoa, so I went up the mast to solve those problems. Going up the mast at sea is a frightening experience and it took me most of a day to solve the problem with the sail, partly due to simply not taking the right tools up in the first place. I heard via radio about Alegre, a much larger boat heading for the Marquesas in French Polynesia. Joan and Gordon had almost the same problem I experienced. The story that came to my ears was that when nudged by his wife Joan to solve the problem Gordon's response was, "I don't care what Mary McCollum did I'm not going up the mast on this boat. We'll make it without a genoa." He did make it and was very helpful to me almost two years later as I arrived in New Zealand.

Next I had to re-install parts of the stainless frame for the canvas spray dodger; I don't remember how it came apart but it did. When that was accomplished I somehow managed to get a line around the propeller shaft and finally got it free, but the worst happened in the middle of the night. My trolling generator tangled with an enormous fish net. If it could go wrong it did go wrong those first two weeks.

That latter encounter gave me a bit of a scare. I didn't want to cut the net and fortunately the owner recognized something was wrong and three small dinghies helped to untangle. I brought the generator in to avoid a duplication of the problem but once everything was free two of the boats immediately departed while one, with several men on board stayed behind. One inquired, "Sola?" (Alone) No, I responded, "Mi esposo duerme."(My husband is sleeping I lied.) They slowly departed but I almost immediately turned out my lights for some time. I just hadn't liked the looks on their faces or the tone of his voice.

The weather had been gray, the winds fickle and currents opposite of predicted so I gave up the first part of the plan, Galapagos, and determined to just continue on to Easter Island, 2000 miles from the nearest population center, one of the most remote populations in the world. Then one day the sun came out. I met the trade winds and by now I had so adapted to life at sea I just didn't want it to end. I never saw or heard sounds or radio signals from another craft so I assumed I was pretty much alone out there.

At dawn on Easter Sunday, 250 Easters after the first visit of a Western ship, captained by the Dutchman Jacob Roggeveen, I was thrilled to see the statues of which I had seen so many pictures through the years. The Island was clearly in view as daylight broke but the famous statues were in view before I could actually make out land formations. While arrival was one of the greatest thrills of my life I was clearly also feeling sad that this journey was ending, having already forgotten those first two weeks.

Mighty Merry Too was a glorious sight arriving into the harbor of Hanga Roa with main sail and a brilliantly yellow, red, orange and purple cruising spinnaker flying but she must have also looked almost like a toy to the only vessels in the anchorage; 6 large tuna boats, on their way north after a discouraging fishing season in the Southern Ocean.

I was greeted on the VHF radio by a gentle New Zealand voice from one of the Tuna boats. "Are you really alone on that little tiny boat?" There lies part of the secret of not being lonely. Everyone does notice when Mighty Merry Too arrives. Few can prevent their curiosity from leading them to inquiries, offers of help and offers of information. All of this allows me to find companionship when desired as well as avoid company of those I prefer to avoid. In this instance the next phrase I heard was, "This is a dangerous anchorage. Let me throw you a line and tie off from my stern." That same gentle voice later insisted on my raiding the freezer on his boat as well as accepting jerry jugs of diesel that he knew were free from contamination. While I never expected to see him again I did indeed see him and his entire family a few years later; not first in New Zealand which was their home, but in Tonga an Island Kingdom that I visited on my way to New Zealand from French Polynesia. Later I also visited their home in New Zealand.

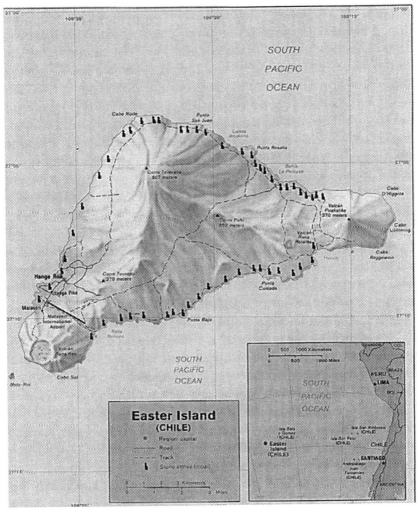

u

The trip to Easter Island was the longest single passage to date; 40 days at sea. During that time I only saw one airplane contrail in the sky and although I did tangle with Ecuadorian fish boats in the first 10 days I never saw another vessel subsequently until arriving in the harbor at Easter Island. While still 700 miles away from that harbor I was very startled to receive a call on the ham radio from the Port Captain at Easter Island, welcoming me to the Island. He had listened to my ham radio conversations with sailors in distant parts of the world. There is no privacy on either the ham or marine single side band radio and both are usable for very long distant communication but neither are there any long distance charges. At times we can carry on conversations covering vast distances. As an example, one day I was talking to my son in Boston and a Japanese physician in Japan at the same time. Those distances are very much controlled by the weather also. I was told that in a really busy year as many as 40 boats came through those waters to Easter Island, compared to the hundreds arriving in French Polynesia. Nevertheless, a week after my arrival, Jim and Shannon on Reefer arrived, friends I hadn't seen since Mexico, so I had companions to share a rental car and tour the more distant parts of the island. Four years later, I missed seeing those same friends by hours as I sailed out of Brisbane, Australia.

Upon arriving the port captain informed me, via VHF, that there was room for me in the small inner harbor, but due to the hazardous entrance I was required to utilize a pilot who would soon be brought to my vessel. I do believe that pilot knew the hazards, of which there were plenty going in, but he seemed to know nothing about the gears of an engine, and wasn't about to listen to a woman, even though she had brought her own vessel all these many miles. I wondered if I would have a working gear shift left after his departure.

I could then clear customs by walking to the port captain's office from where I was. He was very friendly and courteous, stating he would like me to have dinner at his home with his family and would be in touch at a later point to specify a time. Eventually I realized he was probably also very status conscious. He had reason to be down in the inner harbor sometime later and saw my wee little vessel from a short distance. I never heard from him again. After becoming better acquainted with some of the locals I learned that the Chilean officials did indeed see themselves as far superior to most of the residents of the island.

This experience with customs was quite different from most other countries however. Entrance was simple paper work and a few fees while departure required a thorough search of the boat and quarantine on it until the moment of actual departure. Evidently they were more worried about some of their citizens leaving, as well as what archeological token a visitor might be taking with them upon departure. Fortunately I didn't have to use that pilot again.

I also found it curious that the vegetables and fruit purchased at local farm stands were perfectly safe to eat whereas those coming in by ship from mainland Chile required thorough cooking just as I had done in Mexico and in China.

As I frequently did, I joined up with a couple on another American boat to hire a local guide to get a tour of the island. He wasn't a native nor was he a Chilean but had a definite Cockney accent. He also made it clear that he wanted to leave the island but wasn't free to do so. We didn't probe even though curious.

The seasons controlled much of my planning so after a two week visit I continued on to Pitcairn Island almost 1,300 miles from Easter Island. This turned out to be a week's trip in quite tumultuous seas. I was certainly glad that I wasn't dependent on my sextant since the cloud cover meant little opportunity to get a sight with it.

The residents of Pitcairn are the descendants of the mutinous crew on the HMS Bounty and live in one of the most remote societies of the world. There is no adequate anchorage at the Island so I really didn't know how much I would be able visit or see. Upon arrival I noted another quite large sailing vessel at anchor in the most favorable location. Although renamed it was familiar in appearance; I soon learned that was because of it's participation in earlier America's Cup races. I spent a long time circling the area, watching my depth sounder, while trying to find a location where my 200 feet of anchor chain might be sufficient once I got an anchor into whatever lay below. The captain of the large vessel called on VHF to report that he would send a diver over to inspect my anchor once it was down and also that with their quite large crew there were always at least two on board so if and when I went to shore they would keep an eye on MM Too to provide additional safety.

The diver reported that I had probably found the only substantial patch of sand in the area and that the anchor appeared to have dug in very well. The irony of all of this was that when they departed their anchor was caught wedged into rocks and after long efforts their windlass finally broke so they resorted to cutting the chain and leaving the anchor and a good part of their chain behind.

I BELIEVE THIS SPEAKS FOR ITSELF

What a help they were!! Without someone competent watching my little craft I would not have dared to go ashore and I would have felt very cheated to go all that distance and not be able to actually visit. I spent the night, went to shore the next morning, enjoyed the very generous hospitality of those who took me around on a tour of the island, but upon my return I pulled anchor and departed for The Gambier. I really didn't want to remain in an iffy anchorage another night.

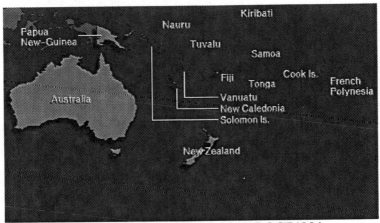

ISLANDS OF THE SOUTH PACIFIC OCEAN 1

The Gambier are the more southerly French Polynesian Islands and therefore most logical next destination from Pitcairn. Few of the hundreds of cruisers going to the South Pacific every year choose the route that would take them to Easter Island, Pitcairn, and the Gambier; few tourists arrive by other means since there are few flights there even by the French airlines. Therefore I expected to see more of local life sans tourists, which indeed I did. There is a hitch to the lack of tourists however; there is no reason for the locals and/or bureaucrats to learn English and I confess to never mastering even a minimal amount of French. I now blame much of this on a hearing loss that perhaps I wasn't aware of then. Today with my very modern hearing aids I might fare better.

So while I found Mangareva, the main island of the Gambier very welcoming and very pleasant I found communication very difficult. Very few people on the island spoke English. My encounter with the port captain was particularly difficult for that reason. I later found in some islands of French Polynesia the bureaucrats lack of English was a put on but here it was very real. Most of my communication was with other cruisers, of whom there were few but they did consist of people I knew quite well by now. There were a very few who spoke French and provided our communication with the local Polynesians who were very welcoming.

The island was charming and it provided good anchorages and the locals urged me to spend Cyclone season there since this archipelago was untouched by cyclones. I also knew the port captain was a person who absolutely stuck to the rules, I knew I couldn't understand a word he said, I didn't believe he understood my English, and I wasn't certain I trusted the translations I was getting from those who tried to help me. Therefore I wasn't sure of my status so with those doubts in mind, I soon continued on to the Society Islands which include the famous Tahiti. There were a number of archipelagos in French Polynesia I didn't visit for a variety of reasons. The Marquesas are considerably north and east of where I entered although this is where the bulk of the cruisers do enter. The Tuamotos would have been en route to Tahiti but simply were too coral infested for a single handed boat to traverse. I've always been a bit envious of friends who did visit them as they were more untouched by modern civilization as well as providing extraordinary snorkeling and diving. I did attempt to go to the Australs when I left Mangareva but the winds were sufficiently against me I simply didn't feel like fighting it; although Shannon and Jim on Reefer, one of the boats that had been at Easter Island with me, did go.

One of the islands used for atomic testing by the French lay between the Gambier and my route to Tahiti in the Society Islands. despite my lack of fluency in French it was made very clear by the French navy that none of us were to come anywhere near that island. One boat I knew did have a serious problem and anchored near it to make repairs but French Naval personnel immediately were there to demand they leave; problem or no problem. I personally did come close enough to it that a navy ship stayed where they kept me in view for half a day. It wasn't a comfortable feeling.

The anchorage at Papeete, Tahiti was well packed with cruising sailboats from many countries. Boats were tied aft to trees on shore with a bow anchor forward and frequently so close together as to need bumpers between us. This was possible only because the tidal changes were minimal but regardless, I found this a particularly uncomfortable situation. When I arrived one of the boats that had helped me back in Ecuador, Watermelon with Peter and Jean on board, was working hard to save a place for me so I did anchor next to them. I stayed only long enough to do what was necessary to clear customs and walk around Papeete to get the feel of the town but during all the time I spent there I felt it was a disaster waiting to happen. While we were inside a reef so we had some protection from the ocean this many boats packed together just didn't seem reasonable. I didn't dwell on those possibilities too long or I would have cut that visit even shorter than I did.

There was also an area where there were docks. These required a reservation far in advance as well as very steep fees. After only a matter of a few hours in Papeete I received a radio call from a boat from that area inviting me to dinner. I was rather startled since I had never met the people nor even heard about them but what could I lose by accepting the invitation? The wife had called and given the invitation and then turned the radio over to her husband who said, "I want to meet you to tell you that you are the reason I am here." I was totally puzzled. He followed it up with, "We were sitting in Fort Lauderdale,

Florida, wondering if I could sail this boat to Polynesia when I read a magazine article about you. I thought if that little 60 year old lady can sail all alone on that little boat to where she has gone than I can certainly sail this magnificent craft to where I want to go."

Well, I was curious about that "magnificent craft" so I did go for a walk earlier in the day of the dinner invitation to see what it was all about. Yes, it was a magnificent craft; large, a pretty design, and exceedingly well equipped. To myself I wondered if I would want to sail that large a boat with just two people. Well equipped yes but in a storm that was a lot of boat and a lot of sail to handle. I guess that says something about perspective doesn't it? It was a most enjoyable dinner and I certainly did see how the other half lived.

Back in Cocos Island there had been a boat with a French couple we all found very strange. They seemed to be living on a shoe string; their equipment was minimal, they seemed to live off their catch from the sea, and their dinghy smelled so bad that none of us would go near it nor did we want them coming close to us. When they prepared to leave they found their forestay was broken and they requested help from Jacques who recruited several other men to help. Jacques insisted they clean up their dinghy before anybody would help. I did have a spare stay stowed away and offered it if they could use it. It's a long story but repairs were made without utilizing the stay I provided, but then they tried to buy the stay from me for a pittance. I refused. The general impression was that they had very little in money or supplies to back them up. A few days after I arrived in Tahiti I heard someone with a French accent shouting to me from shore so I rowed in to try to understand who and what. Who? The Frenchman from the boat I just described, appearing clean and well dressed and through gestures insisting I follow him. He led me a few blocks back away from the beach and pointed proudly to the sign above a large Laundromat. Sure enough: it was his.

After a few days in downtown Papeete I learned about another anchorage that appeared to me much safer, though not in the center of all the festive activity going on downtown; I moved out there.

I had heard repeatedly among the American cruising community that the French would not allow us to spend cyclone season in French Polynesia; thus a year's visa was unobtainable. To date cyclones didn't come into the Society Islands except during an El Nino year and I had no real reason to rush through to New Zealand or Australia, which was the cyclone shelter for most American cruisers. This was not an El Nino year and I did end up spending a full year in the Society Islands, mostly in Moorea or Bora Bora and Huahine. The port Captain from Mangareva was transferred to Huahine so when it came time to obtain permission to spend the extended stay I took care of all the paper work in Tahiti.

I still have such a vivid picture in my mind of the gigantic Polynesian man with whom I dealt. He was not only very tall but gigantically wide. I feared for every chair he sat in. He was equally pleasant, speaking good English and getting a great chuckle out of leading me on with all the possible reasons why my visa application would not be approved while assisting me in making sure I did everything correctly so it would be approved. When I inquired when I might receive an answer his reply was: "Oh, maybe before you die."

Moorea and Tahiti are very close to each other while Bora Bora and Huahine are about 150 miles from Moorea but the trip back and forth was always was a very pleasant sail. I always preferred Moorea as there were good uncrowded anchorages. While in Moorea I was startled one day to see a 104 foot boat come in: the Tam. There were 48 people aboard. It was a 2nd round the world trip for this group, the first having been 20 years before. There were 13 children on board. One from the group celebrated both his 15th and 31st birthday on board. Bob Firestone, the captain told me the history. 20 years previous 4 families got together &

bought first a 65 foot boat, then later a 75 foot and now this 104 foot while keeping the first one. They were centered in the L.A. area and their original goal was to keep their adolescent children away from the drug scene as well as to develop good communication with them in general. They regularly spent Christmas in Mexico. In between these two round the world trips they had also frequently taken underprivileged children with them on special trips to places like Alaska in an effort to help them develop goals and expectations.

Don and Diane flew in to visit again and brought an amazing amount of parts and equipment for me, even including an Avon dinghy. We took advantage of the excellent snorkeling in the Society Islands.

I also took care of much needed dental work in Tahiti where I had no difficulty finding a well trained dentist who spoke good English and didn't seem offended, as so many others were, by my inadequate French. I would suppose my American dollars might have made up for my lack of French. Due to the belief among the American cruisers that one couldn't obtain a visa to remain an entire year there were very few of us here but I did become well acquainted with a number of French and Belgians.

When a Woods Hole research vessel came in to Papeete I received a greeting via VHF. Since I didn't know anyone on board I was astounded but I certainly accepted the dinner invitation that followed the greeting. It was both an entertaining and informative evening. The same thing happened when a Scripps Institute research vessel came in. The ham radio turned out to be the explanation. The ham radio operator on board had listened in, as so many hams do. As I mentioned before there is easy communication over long distances but no privacy.

In Bora Bora I met a group of four young Frenchmen on a boat who all spoke excellent English which was sufficiently unusual that I tried to inquire, courteously I hoped, how that happened to be. Their response was that they knew the French had a reputation for not being willing to do that so once they planned the trip they recognized English would be the useful foreign language to learn. They not only all took classes to learn the language they spoke it on board to provide the practice needed. Instead of traveling through the Panama Canal as most European boats do to get to the Pacific they went around Cape Horn. Why? To save money. Passing through the Canal is very expensive and they were on a tight budget. When it ran out they would have to go back to France and start their careers. They had a rather unique pattern of authority and method of accomplishing what needed to be done. Every job rotated among the four; i.e. one day you were captain, another day you were cook and another day you were clean up and the fourth day you were free of responsibility except to stay out of the way.

It was a pleasant and almost uneventful time period for me with very stable pleasant weather. I celebrated my 63rd birthday there which made me eligible to start withdrawing social security which helped my very pinched budget. Once the cyclone season was over I followed my plan to continue on to New Zealand via Aitutaki in the Cook Islands.

A SUNSET AT SEA

CHAPTER SIX
FEELING LIKE A SPECIAL PERSON

I eagerly departed for Aitutaki, one of the Cook Islands, after a year in French Polynesia. Even though those islands were full of coral which had provided plenty of experience, that year of practice did not increase my confidence: just seeing what happened to a few other boats taught more caution than ever. Safely picking one's way through coral is probably the single most difficult task a single-handed sailor faces. After a few minor scrapes at very slow speeds I had built up a great deal of timidity whenever I knew there was coral in the area. Many sailboats have steps up the mast so that a crew member can get up high to view the coral lying under the usually crystal clear waters. I had steps up the mast that served me well when needing to solve problems up the mast but for this purpose they contributed nothing. after all I couldn't steer the boat from up high in the mast. Actually I did try that one time. I had an electronic autopilot with a handheld remote control so I tested out the possibility and quickly learned it was a futile effort. The auto pilot actually was useful in very limited conditions under any circumstances and this definitely was not one of them. No wind was one of the factors determining usefulness.

Rarotonga is the island most cruisers visit if they visit the Cook Islands and it is a common tourist destination as they do have an airport adequate for aircraft of a size tourists expected. I chose Aitutaki over Rarotonga, (customarily shortened to Raro), for a variety of reasons. knew that the primary harbor at Raro was not at all well protected. Further, the bottom was not conducive to safe anchoring; therefore even though Aitutaki was much more off the beaten path it sounded more desirable. Raro is the capitol of the Cook Islands, which consist of 15 islands, spread out over 770,000 square miles of sea. The total land area of all the Cook Islands combined is only 91 square miles. Let's make a little comparison: back during my summers in Ontario I frequently stopped at Manitoulin Island in Lake Huron, the largest fresh water island in the world. Its land mass is 1068 Square miles.

Raro is much more of a tourist attraction then is Aitutaki, which was another reason it wasn't as attractive to me. The fewer tourists that visit an area the more likely is the opportunity to see island life from the resident's point of view. Raro does provide beautiful scenery; probably much like Hawaii prior to World War Two, in other words, before it became overbuilt for tourists and over inhabited.

The Cooks are self-governing but do have a free association with New Zealand. From what I could gather of that relationship the residents are free to come and go to New Zealand and the Kiwis help them out as needed. It also means that everyone speaks English. The Polynesians generally speak their own language at home but school is taught in English with the result that they all learn English.

Very frequently people ask, "Aren't you afraid out there on that big ocean?" The answer is that most of the time when circumstances are such to cause fear I am too busy dealing with what needs to be done to be conscious of being afraid. This trip provided one of the more frightening nights I remember. As I neared Aitutaki, the seas began to build, and, build, and build. For some reason most of us think of the Trade Winds as consistent gentle breezes. This was my first experience with accelerated Trade Winds, which are consistent but may be gale force and I found to be quite common in that part of the world. It was the first and only time that I went bare pole (no sail up at all), put wash boards in the companionway to prevent water coming in if a huge wave were to come into the cockpit and then I pulled the hatch and locked it. Thus I had locked myself into the cabin. I was making four knots even with no sail. My maximum speed with full sail was normally

6 knots. The wind steering vane however did do its job of taking me away from my destination; necessary because I would have arrived in the dark and the entrance was a tricky and difficult one under the very best of conditions. I had a compass inside so I knew I was keeping the course I had chosen; despite the crashing sounds and howling winds I was keeping a steady course and Mighty Merry was behaving herself in relation to the ferocious waves so I didn't see a need to do the next logical thing which was to heave to. I was reluctant to heave to because of my proximity to the island; I wanted to get away from it.

I was also happy to think about the fact there was very little traffic in this part of the ocean although that was certainly no guarantee that there wouldn't be traffic. The salvation to my nerves probably is that I am the eternal optimist so I didn't dwell on "what if there is another vessel out there." I did, as usual, have my VHF radio on and I would also hope that, as is usually the case, when a ship is in my area I hear some radio traffic or they see me on their radar. The crashing waters all night long were frightening. I make no pretenses otherwise. But frightened as I was I knew I had done everything I could do to protect my craft and myself. Somehow hysteria doesn't seem to be the thing to do when there isn't anyone to pay attention to the hysteria, but it was a long night.

As dawn broke the winds eased, as did the seas. I had heard noises in the night that told me I might find surprises when I went up above and indeed I did. I had a heavy teak platform with a spare LPG bottle attached to it with 8-inch bolts holding it in place. I remember the many comments when installing it in Costa Rica. "It will take a hurricane to tear that out", but the next morning it was gone. That was all the damage that was done but I have always remembered it as the most uncomfortable night I can remember; with one exception and the discomfort of that exception was due to injury rather than fearful seas.

I might have been better off had I hove to but I was uncomfortable doing that simply because I was too close to my destination. Night was falling as I was reducing sail and the best thing to do from my viewpoint was to maintain a course that took me away from the island.

As dawn broke I diverted back to Aitutaki and arrived outside the harbor about midday. As I've already explained, I was very timid entering any new harbor where there was coral; this was the most harrowing entrance I had seen yet. There is a big sand bar between the anchorage and the reef. This sand bar dries at low tide, so about half the day one has a beach just a few feet away in what feels like the wrong direction; i.e. the island was the opposite direction. It was actually very unnerving at first.

I'd had almost no sleep the night before so when I arrived I was not exactly rested and raring to go. I approached the entrance and hung around it, tacking back and forth, for an hour or more, because there was no similarity between what I saw and what the navigation chart showed. Over and over I always remind myself to believe the chart no matter what my eyes think they see. This difference was far more extreme than what my spatial relations disability usually caused. I could see two masts inside. One of them was obviously a boat much larger than mine so I did guess that I could enter but exactly how I didn't understand. Finally a tourist dive boat came out and I radioed to him and he gave me instructions and information that saved me.

Those instructions didn't match the chart and they didn't match the navigation marks placed in the channel but they worked. Later I learned that the chart purchased from the US government only a few months previous showed the entrance as it had been prior to the US Army having blasted it open back in World War II. I now began to understand why some American and British cruisers always purchased French charts that were for this part of the world. The French government, with all of French Polynesia and New Caledonia still being French, simply have more interest in keeping charts up to date. On the other hand it left me a bit antagonistic towards my own government, especially since many charts purchased from them are copies from other country's charts anyway and the price does keep up with inflation so they aren't cheap.

As I came close to the first boat at anchor I saw the owner standing in the water next to it with water only up to his knees. I gulped because I knew my keel was deeper than that. After a lot of effort and assistance from my soon to be neighbor I finally felt secure with two anchors down and I learned to enjoy the fact I had a beach only about two swim strokes away. Regardless of the pleasure of that, with just a little sand over coral where my anchors lay it never felt very secure. That anchor just had nothing to dig into. The two anchors did reduce the spread of my swing so I would stay away from the beach so close by.

As is usual, the minute the formalities were taken care of with customs and immigration, I headed for the post office where my mail was waiting. The customs task was very easy in this instance. The officials were friendly, helpful, not terribly official and most important to me, they spoke English.

The post office visit is always an interesting event in small third world countries. It is often one of the best sources of local information and for the locals a great source of gossip. In this instance I immediately met two American expats, one a Vietnam War resistor from my hometown who had left the US and emigrated to New Zealand, married a Maori woman from Aitutaki and was now teaching math in the local school. The Polynesians from New Zealand and the Cooks are considered Maoris, speak the same language and move freely back and forth from the Islands to New Zealand.

The other American was Barbara, the wife of a Peace Corps volunteer. The first word from each was, "Do you play bridge?", so the weeks in Aitutaki were full of contrasts; much of it spent in local island pastimes with Maori families interspersed with bridge games and American style conversations.

It was also a chance to see our tax dollars at work, i.e. the Peace Corps. What I didn't realize until then is how many other countries have a similar organization. While I don't remember the names of their organization one example was right here: he was a young Australian in the Cook Island's fisheries department. I later met a German medical doctor. Both were from their respective government's third world agency. A few months later in Tonga I met several similar volunteers from England. Barb's husband, Mike, was a retired Iowa farmer teaching the locals to utilize their scant resources more effectively. In some instances it was a case of ignoring the more "modern" practices and going back to some highly effective ancient practices. I had seen the same sort of thing back in Costa Rica.

The Cooks seemed to me to be so different from the Society Islands; partly I'm sure because English is the official language although the native children speak only Maori until they enter preschool and the native families speak Maori among themselves. I actually had a better opportunity to see inside a modern native Polynesian culture for several reasons. While one of those reasons was because of their use of English it is only reasonable to also point out my deficiency. I just never succeeded at learning French and thus probably missed a lot of opportunities in the Society Islands and Mangareva. The other reason was because I had so much opportunity to personally partake in their activities.

Additionally the Cooks and particularly Aitutaki were much more out of the way to the sailing fraternity so visiting sailors were more of an oddity and thus we were more interesting to the locals. Since only very small boats can enter the harbor at Aitutaki visitors were even less frequent than in some of the other Cook Islands, especially Rarotonga and a single-handed woman was a true novelty. While tourism was an important ingredient of their economy there was only one hotel on Aitutaki and the only plane flights were small planes from Rarotonga.

Each of the Cook Islands seemed to have a personality of its own; Aitutaki residents being known for their rather boisterous and fun loving personalities. Tradition has it that when Tahitians wanted to have a good time they set out in their canoes to visit Aitutaki. This was despite the London Missionary Society. It was the first island attacked by the LMS and they really won the natives over in full force. Of course their argument at the time must have been pretty convincing: as the natives were dying off with their first contact with Western diseases the missionaries convinced them the reason was that they were worshiping the wrong god. Mangareva today is predominantly Roman Catholic for exactly the same reasons.

Very quickly I felt exceedingly welcome. Mama is a title of respect among the locals and by the time I left I was regularly greeted as Mama Mary. I did a lot of reef fishing with Ina, the American's wife and there was rarely a day I wasn't given a fresh lei (pronounced ei in this part of Polynesia) and some days two and once even three leis. These actually led to a great deal of personal discomfort. The problem is I don't have that wonderful thick Maori hair and after a few hours the lei really itched my scalp but I didn't dare not wear it for fear of offending the donor. I began to feel there was competition to see who could make the prettiest one for me and I feared if I took it off it might seem unappreciated. Basil leaves, which give off an herbal fragrance I particularly like, made up the greenery in the lei so it was pleasantly aromatic as well.

Tuesday and Fridays afternoons were spent at one of the village playing fields. Life stops at noon on Friday and the netball and rugby games start. They claimed 97 percent of the residents of Aitutaki are active in a sport. I had never heard of netball until then but later learned that more women throughout the world play netball than all other team sports combined. Queen's Birthday (still a celebration of Queen Elizabeth's birthday) was an all day sporting event, starting early in the day with a parade of all seven villages, each in their village playing uniform. I was adopted by the village of Amurri and marched in a borrowed Kelly green skirt, (pretty much like a tennis skirt) and a white and Kelly T shirt with my freshly made pandanus hat and lei.

The parade was at nine and during the parade the runners who had started a race around the island at 7:00 a.m. began to arrive to cross the finish line. At the conclusion of the parade the other events started; everything from discus throwing to races for the four year olds; sometimes two or three events going on at a time but something for everyone including the golden oldies. The seven villages were each competing against each other. The playing field was right next to the market where well prepared lunches were for sale; pig, goat, poke (an island method of preparing paw paw (papaya) with tapioca, breadfruit, kumara (a south Pacific sweet potato.) and coleslaw. One bought a whole pandanus basket full of food, which contained something of everything and was sufficient for a large family. Thank goodness I had that and several other experiences to learn to eat with my fingers. At a later point when I was being treated as the guest of honor receiving the returning seaman's woven palm cape bestowed on me, I needed that knowledge because I had no one to follow. The guest of honor starts first, right? I did giggle the first time I heard a Maori mother tell her children, "now sit up and eat properly, meaning sit at the table, dig in with your fingers and eat.

Included in the day's events were races of the sailing canoes: 27 canoes raced. 10 years previously there were no sailing canoes left on Aitutaki but there had been a revival of the art over the previous two years. For the Easter races there had been 20, 27 for this and enough more under construction there would soon be 50. I was intrigued and pleased by the pride in reviving the old arts. The events ended about

3:00 p.m. and everyone departed for their respective village community center for sandwiches and hot chocolate and much to my surprise a long speech, the only speech in English, thanked Mama Mary for participating.

While I was learning about Polynesian Island life I also was learning more and more about the diversity of life styles to be found among some of the more adventurous Caucasians I met, not just the Peace Corps volunteers, although they certainly qualify in that category. Here on Aitutaki was a relatively young couple who made their living writing and publishing children's books. One wrote and the other drew illustrations. They had no permanent home. Their publishing agent provided them with a mail address. Their portable computer provided them with their office. Each year they chose an activity they wanted to participate in i.e. mountain climbing, skiing etc. and spent a portion of the year where they could do so. Earlier this year it had been skiing in Switzerland. This recreational time was often the more expensive part of their year. Then they chose a pleasant climate in an economy that provided inexpensive living costs, rented a place to live for enough months to write a book, get it to their publisher and move on. In the mean time they also absorbed the local culture and I suspect will or perhaps already have utilized that knowledge in their writing. I accepted one of their current books as a gift intending to take it to a grandchild as a memento but before I had an opportunity for that I ended up in a community where I met a young person working hard to learn to read English. It was also a community where there were few books to be had so I passed it on hoping it would make his task a little easier.

Inside the harbor was a Vaca, (pronounced Waca), a beautiful example of a full size replica of one of the old Polynesian traveling catamarans. Only 12 months previous I had seen the Hukalea, a similar but much larger vessel, come in to Papeete, Tahiti, and Bora

Bora from Hawaii. This voyage was repeating what they believed to be the route and method in which the Polynesians settled the Society Islands. Then I learned that some of the local residents had been on that voyage and were planning to sail this Vaca the 145 miles to Rarotonga, the major island of the Cooks, where it would be used to take tourists out for short sails. There was a problem however. The captain, navigator and some of the crew had been trained in the historic Polynesian navigation skills by a foundation in Hawaii, which has promoted these voyages as a way of maintaining the heritage of their culture. The early navigators spent a lifetime developing their skills but these young men had only a few months of training so we might wonder how these young men could develop enough skills for such a trip. No modern navigation equipment was allowed; a sextant is considered modern.

THE NGAPUARIKI

At the time of my arrival the port captain had hinted that they needed an escort for the Ngapuariki, the Vaca. (The g is almost silent so think of it as Napuariki. Actually it is pronounced with the initial ng sounding like the ending ng in hang but if you can accomplish that it is time for you to go visit the Maoris.) Polynesian society is, in modern terms, very macho and the idea of asking a woman to provide the escort must have been a difficult decision but humans are pretty good at facing reality in almost all cultures. The Rikis, (the town council or circle of chiefs.) decided the favorable time for departure. Originally the Rikis were all navigators themselves but today they are politicians. (Need I say more?) When a departure date was decided the Rikis had to recognize a basic ground rule imposed by modern society: such voyages must have an escort. The next step was to face the reality that the only boat at the island capable of such a journey was the Mighty Merry Too since the other two visiting sailboats were long gone. It was obvious however that even though they overcame their cultural bias to request this single handed woman to escort them there was the need for another person to provide the pair of eyes to keep them in view while necessary boat handling tasks drew the captain's attention away from the Vaca.

Among the people I had met on the island were the couple I mentioned earlier; Barb and Mike on a Peace Corps assignment. They had met in Rarotonga, their meeting having been occasioned by a blackout due to an electrical storm which wiped out the local power system. Barb was a balloonist (hot air balloons) who had traveled the world a great deal; much of her travel was to contests and exhibitions while also working in some of these countries. I had found her bright, compatible and she knew the locals much more than I did so it seemed reasonable to consider asking her if she wanted to come along. She seemed the adventuresome type after all and while she had never sailed she had done a lot of things that required an alert mind, the ability to follow directions as well as think for herself.

I think I actually said something to the effect that I would be happy to do so if Barb were willing to come along as the extra pair of eyes. She happily joined in the new adventure so we set off; later in the day than we would have liked. The delay was caused by all the ceremony required by the full tradition. The Rikis, clergy, and family members all participated in the ceremony. To maintain authenticity to the venture there were no modern navigation instruments on board; not even a compass but there was a VHF radio to be used only in the event of emergency. Our task was to keep them in view at all times, record progress on my chart, as I would normally do for myself and to communicate only if they were more than 50 nautical miles off course.

The captain and several of the crew members were employed by the airline serving the Cook Islands whose home base was in Rarotonga, so news about the trip certainly got around; in fact the flight between Aitutaki and Rarotonga diverted off course to fly low and observe and signal their good wishes. Additionally the local television and radio stations had given the event a lot of publicity, of which I was unaware.

The weather reports had not been auspicious; there was easy access to such information from the airline weather station. Regardless, the politicians had made the decision and the crew and captain of the Vaca all went along with it. It shouldn't have been a big surprise when the weather rather quickly changed. We had made little forward progress when the decision was made to turn around and return home. The problem with that was we would be arriving in the dead of night and if you remember I had found the entrance frightening in broad daylight. I was relieved to learn that one of the crew on the Ngapuariki was employed as driver for the lighter used to unload the cargo ship from New Zealand that delivered supplies to the island. When the cargo ship arrived it anchored outside the harbor in deep water and the lighter worked day and night until all cargo destined for the island was unloaded so he knew the tricky entrance extremely well. The plan was for him to bring the lighter out and tow both MM Too and the Ngapuariki in to the wharf. What I didn't know was that the lighter's fuel supply was extremely low; if it had run out part way through the pass the current was such that we would immediately be on the reef and most likely quickly destroyed. The engine made its last gasps as we were inches from the wharf and able to secure the lines to it.

The next day they helped me take Mighty Merry back out to the anchorage and also showed me a large concrete block with a large ring embedded in it. This block was underwater and I was able to tie off onto it instead of worrying about the anchors dragging in the shallow sand over coral. So, I was ready to re-enter local island life while my little vessel was more secure than ever.

A few days later the supply ship anchored off the harbor entrance. I was really startled to hear the VHF calling to Mighty Merry Too. It turned out the Chief engineer (in charge of the engines) was a young man I had met a few years previously when he had been single handed on a Venture 24, a sweet and hardy little British built sailboat. How did he know I was there inside the harbor? From ZL1MA, Arnold in Rarotonga, who is a real friend to cruisers.

Arnold was our source of weather information via the ham radio in this part of the South Pacific. ZL1MA was Arnold's call sign. There are a number of people in the world I know only by their call sign just as there are a number of people who only know N7ODX rather than Mary or Mighty Merry Too. If you, the reader, are a ham and note that Arnold's call sign doesn't match the Cook Islands it is because he has moved back to New Zealand but is still a very good friend to cruising hams since he now provides more than weather information. As the technology has advanced he is also one of the several angels who forward our email to and from the Internet.

So it was a pleasant surprise to meet up again with the young engineer and also to meet the captain; a woman with some of the worst luck I have ever seen. She and her now deceased husband had done some very adventuresome pleasure cruising on a sailboat. After his demise she had owned and sailed a trading ship through the islands but it was eventually caught in a storm and the ship destroyed on a reef. Now she was captain of this ship and later she was part of a group that bought a retired Japanese training ship; I remember her first cargo was a load of Japanese used cars which were not accepted at their destination. The last time I heard from her the letter included a group of photos of that ship when it caught fire and was lost. She and all the crew were safely rescued.

After renewing acquaintances I began to think of continuing on my journey when I was requested once more to accompany the Vaca on another attempt to get to Rarotonga where the local politicians really wanted to use the Ngapuariki as a tourist attraction. Once more I said, yes, if Barb would also accompany me. She agreed so once more we set off after all the proper blessings by the Rikis. I did know that this time one of the crew had sneaked a compass on board.

During this second attempt we were closer to Rarotonga than to Aitutaki when the weather turned against us once more. The Vaca simply could not make headway and we were required to stay with the Vaca. Then the crew of the Vaca began to get sick and Barbara also became *very* sick. The weather was deteriorating badly and we had been without sleep for a dangerously long time. The crew on the Vaca was wet and cold; they were unable to make headway to their destination and we actually were having difficulty keeping her in sight. The Cook Islands owned one ship, which they used as a rescue and emergency vessel so when finally the decision was made to abort the trip the ship steamed out to meet us all.

Using a large vessel to rescue people off from a small vessel in heavy seas is an impossible task. Using a smaller life raft to do so is not a lot easier; especially when those destined to be rescued are immobilized by seasickness. The only situation I can think of that is as immobilizing as seasickness is a woman in labor. Try if you can to imagine this small craft moving very slowly forward in one direction while the seas pick it up and toss it around in every other direction while at the same moment the life raft (in this instance a very large rubber ducky with heavy outboard motor tries to move in the same direction at the same moment. The wind and waves treat the rubber ducky very differently from the other vessel so that to ever get the two tossing about craft in sync is extremely unlikely if not impossible. The breaking seas are hard on the outboard motor as well. Finally however they got poor sick Barbara rolled over and into the rubber ducky and headed away to the mother ship. There was a ladder down the side of the mother ship but Barb was immobilized and totally unable to maneuver up it. Instead, a very large and strong net was flung over the side, she was lifted and thrown into it and then pulled up to the deck in the net. I didn't see any of the details of how they got the crew from Ngapuariki onto the ship and/or how they got the craft itself attached or loaded on to the ship but it was all accomplished and they set off for Rarotonga while I promised to follow after the weather abated.

I made no promises about when I would arrive and there was so much concern over those being rescued that few questions were addressed to me. The winds were such that I couldn't make a course to Rarotonga even if I wanted to do so. I had a choice of heaving to or finding a safe course and setting the wind steering vane on that course. Heaving to would have been the sensible choice. There was adequate distance between me and any land mass and traffic was almost non existent but the truth is that in my exhausted state it was actually easier to set the wind steering vane and let her go which is exactly what I did. It was a safe course and at that moment I wasn't concerned that it was taking me away from my destination.

Many days later I arrived in Rarotonga on a beautiful sunny day, rested and happy only to find myself very startled at the reception I received.

Dinghies came flying out to meet me; where have you been? What happened to you? How are you? Are you all right? We've been waiting to hold the feast until you arrive.

Where have you been? Four hundred nautical miles as a matter of fact, half of it in the wrong direction. I simply lay down and slept, set an alarm to get up occasionally and check my location and state of the boat but essentially slept for 36 hours until I felt honestly rested. By then the weather had cleared although there was still plenty of wind and the state of the sea was still turbulent and I had put myself in a position that forced me to beat back if I were going to go to Raro. It would have been so much easier to just go on west to Tonga but I had promised to go so I did.

I didn't keep any of my usual radio skeds; partly because I just didn't want my sleep disturbed by that and partly because I didn't want to bother explaining what I was doing. Nobody approves of single-handed sailors despite the fact they serve as interesting curiosities. The result of that is that many single-handed skippers prevaricate about their sleep patterns just to keep the disapprovers at bay. I think some of them even believe their own lies. I couldn't be bothered to lie but I also didn't want to get into a discussion about it. I fully recognize the hazards to single handed sailing. I fully accepted the fact that I might get in to fatal trouble but the rewards were worth the gamble. My greatest fear was becoming a hazard to other boats.

I was more than surprised however by the invitations that awaited me; there was to be a large fete where I was the honored guest. Upon my arrival not only the beautiful hand woven lei of flowers but a palm cape (very heavy by the way) to designate the honored navigator and as the guest of honor I had to be first to help myself to the bounteous banquet on the tables. I was glad I had learned the art of eating with my fingers back in Aitutaki so I wasn't at a complete loss.

All of this of course was provided by the local Maori community but the local television station did get involved and they promised a video-tape of it all that somehow never found its way to me. I heard about it from a variety of people and I know it went through a lot of hands but I never saw it nor could tie down its current whereabouts. I really wanted my grandchildren to see that one.

Part of the ceremony was the presentation of the hero's cape. I don't have the words to describe that cape which was woven in a most intricate and beautiful design from the local leaves and grasses but I shall continue to feel honored even if I can't show it off. It also was very heavy.

Like almost every anchorage I have ever visited Rarotonga was the beginning of many more acquaintanceships and friendships. One couple was contemplating a single handed Pacific crossing on small vessels; plural because they each wanted the experience of the sense of accomplishment such a trip offers. Thus they sought out this single handed woman on her small craft. I met them again in New Zealand a couple of years later after they had accomplished their goal. A contrast was the huge vessel also anchored near my little corner of the harbor; huge to my eyes at least. Only the professional captain and his wife were aboard as the South African family traveling on the boat had rented a house on shore for cyclone season.

They were all avid scuba divers. I had taken a scuba class while in the Society Islands but found the instruction less than satisfactory and never completed it. Once more language had entered into it I am sure but I did want to find out what I was missing in life. It didn't require much more for me to become certified so when the young daughter also expressed an interest in becoming certified we engaged a local instructor. She actually had a good bit of experience diving with her family but was planning to get to the US and or the Caribbean tourist areas where she hoped to find employment and realized the need for proper certification under those circumstances. The instructor was competent and we both earned a license.

Now it was time to move on in order to see the next Island group, the Kingdom of Tonga and then on to New Zealand in order to get there before the onset of cyclone, (hurricane in our hemisphere), season.

CHAPTER SEVEN
BIG DISAPPOINTMENT

Nobody seems to ask the question, "What was your greatest disappointment?" I might hope that has to do with the fact that I don't dwell on disappointments because there are so many positives to think about. In noting those disappointments that I have experienced they are mostly related to a near miss in viewing some of Mother Nature's spectacles. One of the great pleasures of sailing amongst the coral reefs is the snorkeling and diving in comfortable waters. In fact I don't actually like the tropics except for that one feature. To swim in comfort among the colorful residents of the coral reefs is a great joy.

Although certified to scuba dive I generally enjoy snorkeling far more and for this reason actually don't dive that frequently. Additionally, scuba diving requires a partner. The result of these factors tends to create a vicious circle; one needs to dive with reasonable frequency to maintain the required skill. Thus today my certification actually is no longer valid because it has been so long since I dived.

I was in the Kingdom of Tonga, a group of islands west of Rarotonga and east of Fiji, pretty much on the way to New Zealand from French Polynesia. It was a very relaxed time in unusually well protected anchorages in the midst of many cruising boats with lots of acquaintances as well as some close friends. Hurricane protection is so good that the US Navy occasionally uses some of the anchorages.

I had visited an elementary school and tried to explain snow to young children who had never experienced electricity, refrigeration or weather much below 70 degrees Fahrenheit. I will never know how successful that venture was but it was certainly a challenge.

While out at one of the outer fringe islands it seemed a good time to inspect the engine and do any necessary maintenance. It was time to change filters for one thing. Oh, Oh!!!! I discovered water in my diesel tank; a great deal of water. While there were several filters the diesel passed through prior to actually entering the engine it was clear this was more water than these filters could handle. Water was destined to have the engine kill at some crucial moment so the only choice was to find the means to drain all the fuel out, clean out the tank and filter the fuel prior to returning it to the tank. I didn't have adequate containers in which to pump the fuel, all the boats that had been anchored nearby were suddenly gone so there was nobody to borrow from and the whole process became a nightmare that still leaves me exhausted even as a memory. I prefer not to describe it in detail. Although a small tank, (40 gallons), the task required several days because of all the makeshift systems I was forced to use. By the time of completion I smelled of diesel, the interior of Mighty Merry smelled of diesel and I could taste diesel in anything I ate.

After I finally managed to clean myself and my surroundings from the mess I had created and was thinking of leaving the anchorage I received a radio call from a boat I recognized as a local charter boat. Radio calls on the VHF are made from boat to boat in contrast to person to person. That is "Mighty Merry Too, Mighty Merry Too, this is the vessel Duet." The US Coast Guard states exactly how the call is to be made. The requirement is so lengthy that almost no one maintains that protocol. Something of the sort above is most common although most shorten it all the way down to, "Mighty Merry Too, Duet." Many countries have their own requirements for how calls are to be made and often one must obtain a new license while in the territorial waters of such a country. Usually it is a formality designed to obtain a few more tax dollars which in fact it was in Tonga.

The caller identified himself as a member of a group of men on a charter boat, stating they had heard about me and offered a dinner invitation. A few inquiries I made drew out the information that they were all scientists of one sort or another, all worked and lived in different parts of the world although at one time they had studied at university together. Over a period of many years they had arranged to meet annually for a vacation including a common pursuit of some kind. I knew the couple managing the charter boat company and knew they provisioned the galley very well so when the caller stated one of his hobbies was cooking I jumped at the invitation. My supplies were low and probably smelled of diesel and they sounded like an interesting group of people as well as providers of good food.

They were all of that. The food was very good, the wine was superb, and the company very interesting. The plan was to dive the next day and film the underwater experience. The group consisted of an odd number of people, which was awkward for diving. They had extra air tanks, and one of their members held a dive instructor's certificate and would be my partner if I cared to accompany them.. Of course I accepted. It was an especially exciting opportunity since it was a season when a number of whales were known to be in the area. Then I accepted just one more glass of that very good wine before going home for the night, planning to meet them tomorrow at a very early hour with wetsuit and dive equipment in hand.

I will never know if it was that extra glass of wine, eating food much richer than was my habit, contaminated food (unlikely) or just the result of all that work with the smelly diesel but a few hours before our scheduled time to meet I became violently sick to my stomach and was forced to call and say I just couldn't make it. There was much commiseration but nothing to be done about it.

A few hours later as I was beginning to recover I received another radio call from them; the dive had been the most extraordinary imaginable. They had not only seen a whale; they had watched that whale give birth. I still am on the edge of tears when I think about the experience I missed. They did promise me a copy of the videotape they made of it but I never received it. I did have their names and addresses but that was part of what got destroyed in the one fairly serious accident I will soon describe in the next chapter. So guys, if you read this I would still love to see that tape.

From Tonga I went on to New Zealand where I spent a season before continuing on to Fiji. From Fiji I departed much sooner than expected with quite unhappy consequences. That story follows in the next and last chapter of this little tale.

Mighty Merry Too's arrival in New Zealand was not without drama. I don't honestly remember the reasons I used the engine as much as I did, but as I neared the entrance to Opua, my destination for clearing customs, I was without fuel. I was out near the "Nine Pin", a well known landmark, when I was informed that I was required to tie up at the custom's dock. No anchoring was allowed until customs had searched the vessel for contraband. There was no wind and I simply wasn't able to maneuver. In many of the island countries I would have anchored and then dinghied in to shore and walked to customs; not allowed New Zealand.

Gordon, on Alegre offered to bring fuel out to me but he was forbidden to do so. So what did they want me to do? Turn around and go back to Tonga or divert and go to Fiji? When and if the wind came up that is. None of those options were reasonable since it was late spring or early summer in the southern hemisphere and cyclone season was beginning. A primary purpose in entering after all was the fact that historically New Zealand was cyclone free.

Those were my thoughts but, for a change, I was smart enough to keep those thoughts to myself. Gordon on the vessel Alegre, via VHF, convinced customs that if he brought a jug of diesel to me he would pass it across to Mighty Merry Too without touching me or the vessel and was finally given permission to do so. He promptly followed that permission up with action.

Immediately after receipt of the diesel there was a painstaking task waiting for me. Bleeding the engine was necessary after running out of fuel; the fuel lines to the injectors might contain air which would cause the engine to stop dead at some unexpected moment, if it started at all that is. Another problem was the reality that bleeding the engine is not only a painstaking job but it usually means I get pretty filthy. I really didn't want to make that kind of an entrance, especially after this much drama. I knew a multitude of people were listening in to all of this on the VHF.

The job involved opening up various valves to let the air escape as fuel was being pumped. It was easier than it had been in past instances because of the repair way back up on Vancouver Island by the machinist who was ready to retire. While it had been a "jerry rigged" repair it actually made several steps more efficient and had lasted all these years since. Somehow I got it done and cleaned myself up enough to feel I could continue on in.

Customs was pleasant and easy to deal with when I finally got to their wharf. They were very conscious of not wanting any foreign bugs or vermin into the country so all fresh produce was confiscated. I had hard boiled my fresh eggs prior to arrival so I was allowed to keep them.

I was almost immediately befriended by June, a local resident who made it a habit to befriend single handed sailors, be they male or female. I was the first female for whom she had occasion to do this. Befriending included taking me to Whangarei, the closest good sized town for shopping expeditions. Whangarei (pronounced Fangarei) was also a frequent destination for cruisers to enter the country but was a more difficult entrance with no adequate anchorage after clearing customs. There were lots of docks but no anchorage. This led to lots of communication between the cruising boats but not necessarily with the local community. In Opua the local Yacht club hosted all the cruising boats so communication was quickly established between locals and cruisers.

Back in Seattle during the time period I had been outfitting Mighty Merry Too I had become acquainted with a couple, Bud and Peggy, who were doing the same but with the view of relocating to New Zealand. Although Bud was originally Canadian he had sailed and worked in the southern Pacific Ocean and had already purchased property on the North Island of New Zealand previous to his marriage to a Californian woman.

The Yacht Club made it a practice to serve a large Thanksgiving dinner on our American Thanksgiving since there were commonly so many American boats there at this time of year. It was used as a form of welcome. I was not surprised when I saw Bud carving the turkey although he was obviously amazed when he saw me. He stopped carving when he saw me in the buffet line while his mouth dropped open. The line stopped for some minutes while he quizzed me about my travels from Seattle to here in New Zealand. He and his wife also befriended me from that time forward during my stay in the country.

I also learned that in this part of the world all sailboats were either dinghies or Yachts whereas in my experience in the US the word Yacht defined a very large luxurious boat. To speak of one's own boat as a yacht felt very ostentatious but I made it a habit to adapt to local custom whenever reasonable.

By now I did have a plan to spend the cyclone season in New Zealand and following cyclone season to sail to Fiji. Once more friends from the US flew in to visit me. Mary, who had met me back in the Queen Charlottes and I toured the country together; mostly by the very good bus system. Despite having a schedule to meet, the bus driver would stop any time we requested him to do so to look at something we saw something of interest along the way. Sometimes it was only a flower, tree or unusual formation and more likely than not he would also give us a good bit of information about it. He also delivered a few newspapers along the way as well as some fresh bread to be sold in some of the very small stores in the very rural areas through which we might be traveling.

Most frequently we stayed in Youth Hostels. Both New Zealand and Australia are dotted with a great many Youth Hostels, part of the international organization, and provided a very interesting view for us as there were young people from all over the world utilizing the system as well as seniors on a budget like us. Rooms ranged from very basic individual to dormitories. While the youth, usually traveling on an even tighter budget, made full use of the kitchens in the hostels we did favor use of the local restaurants. The youth also tended toward the less expensive dormitories while we chose a little more privacy. One of our most amusing evenings in a hostel was in Dunedin where a large group of young Japanese was spending time. To our surprise the young men did all the cooking.

Shortly after that tour I found myself back in Opua and the Bay of Islands watching the America's Cup trials taking place I also did a good bit of exploring North Island anchorages of which there were many with lots of clams available for the digging as well as oysters and mussels.

I didn't consider exploring the South Island by sail simply because before long it was the season to depart for Fiji, if I were going to go, and it was decidedly in my plans. It was only great luck that the day I chose to depart helped me arrive in Fiji at the outside edge of one of the monstrous storms of the century; the Queen's Birthday Storm. Whole books have been written about the Queen's Birthday Storm and I had a number of friends who were in the midst of it instead of the outside edge as I was but my last hours before arrival were bad enough. If you really want to learn more about that storm I will refer you to: *Heavy Weather Sailing, 30th anniversary edition, McGraw Hill.* One boat in particular that I remember suffered very badly but did not roll as did so many other boats. It was a boat that always seemed in need of so very much maintenance but they made it through that horrendous storm. I frankly was surprised that in late winter of 2005 they completed their circumnavigation of the world and arrived in San Francisco.

I never learned to be comfortable in Fiji simply because of the coral. I loved the snorkeling, some of the most colorful I have ever seen, but once in a secure anchorage I almost never moved until I could follow another boat. An extra pair of eyes is just absolutely necessary in waters with as much coral as is found in Fiji.

Life is full of surprises where ever you are, or another way of putting it is if I wanted to run away from my past I probably couldn't do it. One day I received a message that a colleague from Oakland Community College (my employer before my retirement) was in Suva and would like to come visit me. He had been in Thailand where he frequently spent his summer vacations.

I was at the Trade Winds, an anchorage near Lautoka, some distance from Suva and I don't honestly remember how he got to the anchorage but he did so. I welcomed him with a chicken dinner roasted in my oven; or I tried to do so. I had found the quality of the chickens purchased in the local stores to be exceptionally good so I was trying to show off just a bit as to what could be accomplished on such a little craft. It was a beautiful and aromatic sight as it came out of the oven. One problem; as I pulled it out, trying to be careful to save the juices in the pan for gravy, the chicken slid around in those juices and finally completely out of the pan to the floor. So much for trying to show off.

For me it was an interesting afternoon as I heard lots of details about so many of my former colleagues of whom I had heard almost nothing since my retirement.

The anchorage was rather unusual. I actually had a mooring tucked into a cozy little bay that was highly protected from weather from all directions. In that same bay there were two house boats on moorings. I hadn't seen anything quite as handsome since those in Seattle. Renting and living in one of them was an American Peace Corps volunteer from Texas. She was working with farmer's way up in the hills and frequently brought me produce from some of those farms. Included in the treats she brought were the tastiest tomatoes I had had in many years. I've never had that quality since. They were as I remember the tomatoes from my childhood.

She explained that I hadn't had anything like those in the US because through the years tomatoes were developed to ship well. These tasteless tomatoes are available 12 months a year. Her point was that one can simply not buy seeds that would produce the same quality. Only a few people in the US were clever enough to have seen it coming and saved seeds from their own gardens through the years and thus were still producing quality for their own eating.

Several friends that I hadn't seen since Tonga also arrived and joined me in that anchorage. We discovered a bus came very close by which would take us in to the Royal Suva Yacht club. I was always a little uncomfortable after noting that the main prison for the country was very close to the Yacht Club but that was where my mail was arriving. Also it was the route into the town where a wide variety of restaurants were offering high quality and extremely inexpensive food. We settled on a favorite where we frequently ate lunch; a huge meal of Indian style food for $1.50 when converted to US dollars.

Almost all the commerce in Fiji is Indian or Caucasian while the native Fijians resented the Indians in particular. Commerce would have stopped dead if they were to all leave. They also all speak English. At that time the Indian population had little say in the representative government of Fiji which provided a lot of controversy.

There was a best time of day to shop: if you were the first customer for the day in the store it was deemed very important to the owner thatyou purchase something as that would insure his luck for the rest of the day. If you left without a purchase it doomed his luck for the day. You guessed it. Prices became very negotiable at that moment. I have been followed down the sidewalk as the price is lowered and lowered to entice me to purchase. I learned to not enter stores early in the day unless I was intending to purchase. Why feed the owner's superstition?

I did spend time in some of the villages where housing was as primitive as story book pictures showed South Sea Islander homes. Their overall style of living was equally primitive. In one village in particular I remember there were at two men who had served in the military in the Gulf War but after that broad experience were content with the primitive life in the village. But they just didn't want those Indians to be making all that money.

In that same village there was a telephone which was to serve the whole village but it was unusable because the charges for using it hadn't been paid for such a long time that the phone company had cut them off. This was the same village that was determined to convince me to marry one of their single men. It just wasn't reasonable for a woman to remain single and even more unreasonable to sail her own boat despite the distance I had already done so. In fact several times I was a dinner guest in homes where I realized the intent was to get me together with a single male of the family.

Thank goodness I did find some friends Dave and Kara with grandson Chad on Karabee who enjoyed the snorkeling as much as I did. They were very gracious about my following them to locate some of the more isolated reefs as I didn't dare search these out by myself. I really didn't want to learn the hard lessons to be learned about coral reefs: I repeat that in my mind it is the single most difficult task a single handed sailor faces.

I did make a return to the Yacht Club on occasion to retrieve mail which I was having sent every other week. Then one day I received bad news via that mail delivery which leads to a traumatic story although it is also very funny in places, especially years later when I am strong and healthy again.

It starts as a tale of insurance. I had been insured all along and needed to be. That's another long tale but just take it on face value it was a necessity; it had never been a problem even though single handed. The insurance was through a company arranged by the Seven Seas Cruising Association although that group never acknowledged their role in this issue. Seven Seas is an association made up of experienced cruising sailors. Membership as a Commodore is by recommendation only and one must have accomplished a certain amount of offshore cruising to be eligible. Non Commodores may join and many do so to obtain the information provided by their newsletter. Only Commodores have voting privileges. I have long since resigned my Commodore membership in that association.

In this latest mail delivery I learned that the insurance company, United Community, was in trouble, the State of New York was taking them over and the State ordered that all policies were to be cancelled. I was told by Robert Kidd & staff, agent for AW Lawrence, (which owned United Community) that all premiums would be refunded, all claims paid and if United Community couldn't pay them then the State of New York would do so.. Not to worry. They didn't even know when the cancellation date would be but the policy would be cancelled and they would all be the same date. Would I let other cruisers in Fiji know the situation? Indeed I would and did.

I spent a lot of time in Suva, Fiji looking for an alternative. Early September I received the cancellation notice; effective midnight September 27. I finally found coverage from Lloyd's (whom everyone I knew had said won't cover a single handed boat) but relevant to my budget it was outrageously high so the decision I finally made was to depart almost immediately because, after all, I had a deadline.

THE WEATHER IS CHANGING

CHAPTER EIGHT
NEVER TRY TO BEAT A DEAD LINE

I knew full well it was too early to expect a good weather pattern but I would get to New Zealand before 9/27, the deadline date I ultimately received, and obtain coastal insurance there at about 10 % of the Lloyd's figure. This would give me time to take care of other matters so I could just not insure in the future. In the meantime I put a bank check to cover the Lloyd's policy in the insurance broker's hands with the agreement it would not be deposited until the 27th and then only if they hadn't heard from me by then.

I knew I needed a new main sail. I had one ordered in New Zealand as a matter of fact, to be ready for my scheduled November return. As I left I realized I needed a new Staysail too. I reinforced the leech with a strip of new fabric and hoped. Well, hope just didn't do it. I was making perfectly reasonable progress using trysail and staysail much of the trip which says right there that I had plenty of winds but the closer to New Zealand the more unfavorable the wind direction became. Friends have recently reminded me that for many days I reported on the radio I was experiencing absolutely glorious sailing. My log is lost to water damage so I can't verify but assume that is correct. The part I remember is when the wind picked up and I resorted to heavy weather sails. The following account is a letter I wrote to family and friends a few months after the event. If some of it is a bit garbled this is exactly as I wrote it at the time. That which is in caps is an addition or clarification I have made since.

On the night of the 22nd, with trysail & staysail up the staysail blew to shreds. I mean shreds!!!! I tried to tie it off on the lifelines and it was hopeless to gather the shreds together sufficiently so I ended up cutting it off at the clew and let the shreds go overboard. (I'M NOT SURE WHY BUT THE CLEW AND THE SHEETS WERE STILL TIED TO THE LIFELINES MANY MONTHS LATER.)

The jib was also torn at the clew and unusable but not destroyed. Of course the wind was on my nose and I was breaking (for the first and last time) my primary rule, which is to not try to beat a deadline. So I started motor sailing with the trysail and of course then couldn't use the wind vane so I resorted to the auto pilot. (I still don't think the knockdown would have happened had I been using the wind vane. I've been in much worse wind and much worse seas although these were mightily confused.)

I pulled out my Pete Sutter spare jib (PETE HAS SUBSEQUENTLY DIED BUT WHEN HE WAS A SAIL MAKER HE WAS FAMOUS FOR THE STRENGTH OF THE SAILS HE MADE. HE MADE SAILS AS HE WANTED THEM WHEN HE CRUISED AND HE DID USE THE LAST YEARS OF HIS LIFE TO CRUISE.) This jib had gotten me from Pitcairn to Tahiti when I lost my Genoa. I spent much of the night trying to sew kiwi slides on it so I could use it with the furler.   The problem wasn't sewing them on but hacking off Pete's oversized hanks. The only way was to saw them off one by one and at the rate I was going the whole thing was going to be a 24-hour job.

Of course a perfectly legitimate criticism is that if I considered that my emergency jib I should have had it prepared to use prior to leaving New Zealand in the first place. It really isn't Mother Nature that does us in so much as our own un-preparedness or poor judgment that allows Mother Nature to sneak in on us.

The wind seemed to ease off a bit and I wasn't making any headway so I dropped the trysail and raised the double reefed main which did help a bit although it was rough and slow. Gary, single-handed on Champagne left a few days after me. He had asked, "How many days later than you do I have to leave to arrive the same day as you, Mary? Let's sail in to Matauwhi Bay together and drink champagne." We talked on the radio every day and I talked to Ritchie on Russell Radio every day and I talked to Roy and Joanie on Moorea everyday. Just a jabber box, I am. This time a lot of people knew approximately where I was.

I had promised Gary we were going to get a wind switch to the north as my birthday present, the 22nd. Well, when it didn't come on the 22nd of this hemisphere then I figured since I was born in the US it would be on the 22nd there; the 23rd here.

It was a spectacular sky during the night; not pretty, just spectacular. The full moon was reflecting off from the banks of black clouds even though hidden behind them. Just before dawn I saw something I had heard about but never before seen: a moon bow; a strange olive green. I almost didn't believe they really happened prior to that. About 6:00 a.m. I decided the wind was beginning to pipe up and maybe I should drop the main and put the trysail back up so I put on my harness and was standing on the ladder. I was only seconds from turning to the snap and releasing the halyard before going up to the mast with the trysail. It was at my feet in the cockpit.

Then it happened. The boat laid completely over on her side. When she laid over I was thrown from the top step of the ladder into the cabin to the galley stove where I hit the safety bar around the stove. I think the fractured vertebrae were from the safety bar on the stove. The broken cheekbone and all the rest of the bruises and blood??? I don't know. I did get into the cockpit once because I released the halyard and I saw the mast and sail in the water and saw the sail come up in useless shreds. The dodger frame had pulled loose and the solar panels were flying around so I managed to push them overboard so they wouldn't kill me; saying as I did it, "there goes a thousand dollars."

The radio was all tuned for the morning sked with Moorea. It wasn't long before I realized I was pretty helpless; I can't say I really feared being knocked down again, or rolling. (Rolling would mean the boat did a 360. She was designed to come back up if that should happen but it is always a terrible experience.) For some reason I didn't think it was going to happen. I just knew I was physically incapacitated. I knew the batteries were topped off from the night's motoring. The electric bilge pump worked and I did pump out a lot of water. I could see the Ample Power controller/regulator was not reading so probably was not working and therefore there would be no more charging.

I can't pull out from my memory anything about the engine except that I knew it would start and run and I knew I still had fuel sufficient to get me to my destination under favorable conditions. Much of the electrical system was not working but some was.

I put out a pan pan call with no response (6 alpha I think) (WHICH WOULD HAVE BEEN SINGLE SIDEBAND RATHER

THAN HAM.) I was lying on the sole with the mike clutched in my hand and realized I shouldn't try changing channels but just wait for the sked with Moorea. Don, on Bag End, actually came up first so I told him I needed help and asked if he could get hold of Ritchie of Russell Radio.. Shortly thereafter Taupo radio came up (the New Zealand Marine Safety) and they were there every twenty minutes thereafter except that night when I insisted on turning the radio off against Taupo radio's wishes.

Gary was a prince. He was the perfect person to be communicating with in that kind of emergency; of course he's had plenty of experience. He was in charge of rescue and salvage for the US navy in Pacific. Gary is pure understatement with a wonderful sense of humor to round it out. I remember when they finally said they were sending the helicopter, I told Gary I needed his advice; I realized I would have to abandon Mighty Merry Too and I couldn't leave her out here as a hazard to everyone else but I couldn't think what I needed to do to scuttle her which is a demonstration of just how helpless I felt. How to sink a boat just isn't a problem. Open any valve and leave it open. I can honestly say it is the first time in my life I remember a sense of no willingness to try. It is easy enough when I think about it now but he jumped in immediately, "Don't even think about it Mary. You don't have to think about it. There are all kinds of people ready to come and take care of the boat." Then it became clear that the helicopter was bringing a crew. I had no real idea what was going to happen or how it would take place. IN THE YEARS SINCE I HAVE BEEN ASKED AND I HAVE PERSONALLY WONDERED WHAT I WOULD HAVE DONE AND HOW I WOULD HAVE REACTED HAD I BEEN IN A PART OF THE WORLD WHERE SUCH A RESCUE WAS AN UNLIKELY EVENT; BETWEEN EASTER ISLAND AND

PITCAIRN FOR INSTANCE. I DID AFTER ALL HAVE PAIN KILL-ERS ON BOARD (RIGHT UNDERNEATH ME) AND A LOT OF EMERGENCY EQUIPMENT. IF I KNEW RESCUE WAS OUT OF THE QUESTION MIGHT I NOT HAVE REACTED DIFFERENTLY? I DO THINK SO BUT OF COURSE I'LL NEVER KNOW.

I knew they had determined they wouldn't use a board or a stretcher; I could move my feet, I had stood up at least twice. Actually the pain was from the middle of my back to the middle of my front so I believed I had broken ribs rather than vertebrae and that is what I reported. I knew the plane would come first, followed by the chopper about 30 minutes later What I didn't know was that I was at the absolute outer fringe of their fuel range and that they had not done this maneuver with a small boat before. In fact there is a whole lot I'm glad I didn't know until much much later because in many ways it was a comedy of errors.

They had given an ETA of about 1:30 for the plane but it was actually almost four when the chopper got there. The plane arrived and it was a happy sound as it circled and circled and circled. My VHF was out so I couldn't talk to them or the chopper. When I heard that very distinctive noise (the first time I have ever liked it) I remember smiling and I managed to pull myself into a position where I could at least see it to confirm what I heard. But suddenly I heard a terrible noise, (the winch wire from the chopper tangled in the rigging of MM Too) and then another awful noise (the paramedic land-ing on the bow from about 2 meters above it.) With that I pulled myself into the cockpit and this big klutzy guy in heavy black boots, mustang suit and a helmet clomped around the edge of the dodger and said "hello, I'm Bruce, the paramedic. They broke the wire and can't take us up. I'm stuck here with you, can you navigate?????" and then he promptly puked and continued to do so for the next 20 hours.

At this stage it is terribly funny. But poor Bruce. He had done practice rescues but never a real at sea rescue. He isn't a seaman. He is the sweetest guy but he is a klutz on a boat. I thought I was exaggerating until I heard Steve and Craig describe him; "my god, here you were black and blue, swollen and blood all over and every time he moved he either stepped on you, or tripped over you and then finally he took that heavy medical kit and in the middle of the night dropped it right on your bruised and bloody face."

He came from land to a sailboat with no sails, rolling around in a miserable sea with no helm and he had no idea what state I was in so to question if I was capable of navigating was a very legitimate question.. Anyone would have been seasick in those conditions but then add the fear factor that had to have taken place when the winch wire broke and he knew what I didn't; they could only afford ten minutes at this end due to fuel consumption.

There wasn't time to think about all that however; the chopper was back and hovering very very close, (I had made it into the cockpit I think.) With the door open a man in foul weather clothes (not a wet suit) jumped into the water and swam to the boat; knowing that if he didn't make it there was no way to rescue him. (As he now describes it however, he knew he would make it or he wouldn't have jumped.) MM Too was rolling so that he almost rolled onto the boat. With a broad grin he introduced himself as Craig, a sailor who would get MM Too back to Opua, New Zealand and a moment later a second man did the same thing, introduced himself as Steve and the chopper was gone.

I'm going to use a code here; when I switch to italics it is what they knew and I didn't know. *(The plan had been to have them jump into the life raft. There wasn't a life raft and even if there was it was a plan designed to break more bones on more people if not kill them.)* I was already back down on the cabin sole, Bruce was already on the windward settee (most uncomfortable side) in the fetal position and Craig announced from the cockpit, "well, the first thing we'll do is tidy up down below and then we'll get this ship underway," Then, very slowly, "Oh, no we won't. We'll just get it underway." You just can't imagine how chaotic this little cabin appeared with a puking giant in the windward (high) settee and me wincing on the sole (floor) with every cushion and sundry other item totally out of place and soaking wet. (I later learned that Craig believes I did actually roll. If so it isn't quite as terrible an experience as I thought it would be but I don't believe I did..)

It was a hastily put together plan and I'm glad I wasn't aware of the flaws. Gary's comment was, "I always wanted to meet a real hero and you have two of them on board.", meaning Craig & Steve. It was a very true statement. They are seamen however. They do and have done a lot of deliveries, seem to like to do that together. In fact in the dead of night I remember Steve & I talking about the Grosse Pointe (Michigan) Yacht Club where he spent some time on a boat he delivered. Craig has a yacht services business & Steve has a rigging shop in Auckland. It is clear to me that his employees think the world of him, which speaks volumes. He has also been a sail maker but says rigging is lot more fun.

The night wore on; slowly for all of us. I just hurt; a lot. Bruce was sea sick, compounded I'm sure by the sense of failure; "I'm supposed to be helping this woman and I'm so sick I can't even get out the morphine to give her the shot I keep offering her." Can't you see what that cycle would be like?????

Craig and Steve had to have been desperately cold. (And a bit sea sick too. The first day at sea is like that even in decent conditions. These were not decent conditions.) The decision to jump was so fast and spontaneous there was no preparation. I really was worried about them developing hypothermia. They kept saying, "Don't worry about us. We're young and healthy." Always with a grin. The Pete Sutter sail did come through; they wrapped up in it and it was heavy enough it did give them some protection.

The chopper did return about 1:30 the next day after having dropped barrels of fuel at North Cape as well as dropping seats, oxygen and whatever they could figure out to lighten it up at Keri Keri.. The plane arrived first, circled and dropped, a long ways away, a big package wrapped in bright yellow plastic; the dry clothes I had asked them to bring to Steve & Craig. When the package was retrieved the plastic was split and the whole thing full of water.

The chopper also dropped packages: a staysail, a trysail, (I had told them on the radio I had a trysail; not realizing it had gone overboard during the knockdown) jerry jugs of fuel, and after all of that it was time to take me off. Bruce had rehearsed me thoroughly on what would happen; he had his big harness on again, they slipped a strap under my arms and helped me into the cockpit. The winch wire would be attached to Bruce and I would be attached to Bruce, facing him, slightly below him. The wire came down and suddenly was attached to me, I was yanked and up I went, by myself. (Bruce believed that I wasn't attached and would fall,) Thank god I didn't know that for a long long time.

I also didn't know that I was the subject of a news bulletin on both television and radio in New Zealand, every 30 minutes throughout the whole ordeal. Kiwis were so sick of my name that I had to do my part in the hospital and say thank you to them in all those radio and television interviews. (Just this afternoon I saw some friends for the first time since their return from London, where they live most of the year. Wayne said she read about me in the London Times as well as in the clippings from the N.Z. papers which Kiwi friends had sent.

I got out of the hospital on the 26th (remember, the deadline was the 27th.), stopped at an insurance broker, got a binder for local insurance and immediately called and had my check to Lloyd's returned.

I also called AW Lawrence to report the claim, learned that the broker didn't want anything more to do with me even if he had gotten his commission all those years, learned there was no rush on getting the claim in as they haven't paid a claim since July and who knows when and if they ever will. Oh. "And by the way, don't ever call us again."

I finally have acknowledgment that they accepted a claim for over $17,000 US, after the deductible they acknowledge they owe me $10,040.07 US but won't be paying me. The State of New York will only pay, from their guarantee fund for New York residents who were not more than 3 miles off shore. All other claims will be sent to the claimant's "residence of record." and wherever I am a resident doesn't pay marine claims from their guarantee fund.

They are in "rehabilitation". Essentially, the State claims the insurance company is insolvent and they claim they are not so the State will not allow them to pay claims or write any business and they are battling in court. If they are liquidated before they use every thing up in lawyers and CPA fees then there might be a partial payment at least but if it ever happens it is likely to be years.

Now, here is the clincher. When arrangements were made for Steve and Craig to come the man that made the arrangements was told that the government would pay for it. (They called a salvage company and he paid Steve & Craig.) When the Marine Safety Office investigated the incident he asked me if I had insurance and I said yes but that the company was in bankruptcy so I might never get anything. The salvage company submitted the bill, $2500, (which is a pittance really) and the government refused to pay it on the grounds that I am insured and should be the one to pay it so I indeed do have the bill and it has been submitted to the insurance company. I have also heard things like "I would hate to have to get a lien on your boat to prevent you from leaving the country"

So there is my tale.

Now, to the future rather than the past. What are my plans? Well, I am going to get myself healthy. I did fracture a vertebrae or two; T5 & 6 I guess. The orthopedic surgeon has lectured me about I should consider a different life style; the x-rays didn't look good so I had a bone density (the first I've had) and it wasn't good; 2 deviations below the mean for my age so I am on hormone replacement therapy. He says there is a lot of osteoporosis. The GP says why that should mean I should change my life style. (The GP is a woman from Texas.) (OF COURSE THIS

LETTER WAS WRITTEN A LONG TIME BEFORE THE AWARENSS OF THE NEGATIVES OF THIS THERAPY.) A lot is happening with treatment for Osteoporosis right now so there is some hope for improvement although I may be just a few years too early. I've had a good bit of arthritis these last few months. The GP says that goes with early menopause (which I did experience) and often triggered by trauma. I didn't move back on board MM Too until December 6 and I must say I was much improved almost immediately upon doing so. I have always experienced a lot more joint pain when on land for extended periods so I presume it is the constant, even if slight motion that the body has to adjust for all the time when on board.

Admittedly it was a spectacular December here, which certainly helped. At present I am slowly getting MM Too together but paying more attention to trying to get myself plenty of exercise, of a suitable kind i.e. strengthening but not damaging. My knee was pretty bad, one thumb absolutely useless and one finger on the other hand pretty bad. My neck gets fairly bad sometimes. I thoroughly enjoy walking anyway and the terrain is such there is no difficulty in finding spectacular scenery and elevating the heart rate with the required effort. I'm rowing since I don't have a motor now anyway (the port side went over and the motor was on the port side. Some days rowing is a very easy task but on those days I make several trips resulting in at least three miles a day while other days when the tide is flowing hard and/or the wind velocity is 30 knots it requires a fair effort. I have a mooring at Matauwhi bay, Russell. It is deep enough into the bay it is protected from all directions and the setting is lovely. Can hear Kiwis at night, look at a pair of palm trees on the beach and bush all the way up the slope.

My son Mike is planning to come to New Zealand to visit and so is Annabelle so I don't plan to go to the States for a while longer and I am expecting several friends.

My finances have been in great disarray because not only have there been the expenses of MM Too repairs but I've had to foreclose on a land contract back in Michigan which meant less money coming in and much more going out but most of that has now been sorted out so I can begin to plan again.

MM Too is habitable (the electrical system got almost entirely re-done in December. It is on the port side too.) And is sailable due to very generous locals. A lot has been done already; rudder repaired, new tiller made & installed & dodger frame fixed. The mast was off being repaired and I was without it a month and obviously uncomfortable!!!!   Now the mast is repaired, and has new rigging, the jib is repaired and I have a borrowed main (from the maintenance man at the local school) and I don't need either a stay sail or a trysail for playing around here in the Bay of Islands where there are so many delightful places to go.

I do expect to continue on but I do not plan to leave this year. I also plan to do more cruising in New Zealand before I leave so that makes it May of '96 I guess.

I have talked with other single handed people; wondering what might have happened if this had happened, say between Easter Island and Pitcairn. There wouldn't have been help available and I wonder. I remember the sense of not being able to help myself, not being able to make the effort. That is the most painful memory of all. Well, of course I can't know but I do know the human tends to respond to necessity; if I knew there could be no help would I have found a way? Maybe.

Craig and Steve are very different personalities. Craig, younger and a born flirt I'm sure. (Craig tells the story that when Ritchie asked him if he wanted to take on the recovery he asked, what's involved? Ritchie told, him well it's a 64-foot boat (everybody knew it was my 64th birthday) and a 24 year old single handed bimbo. (Ritchie laughs very hard and then denies the story but acknowledges he told Steve it was a very little boat. When Steve asked "How little?? "You don't want to know."

Steve doesn't say much but when he does it is very much to the point so when he told me, "Mary, I don't care if you have to be rescued 3 more times. If you want to go, go." I found it most reassuring. Coming from the man who risked his life for my boat I guess I can afford to take his comments seriously.

I was most overwhelmed by Bruce. He has made a lot of effort to stay in touch. He called me one day and just poured his heart out; he made me feel like the hero. He's been back on the boat. I had guests for dinner that night but I'm hoping he will give me just a little warning next time he is in this part of the country as I would like to have him and his family for dinner. I think he needs that. So there you have it.

But there is a finale to this story. Friends in many countries were so very gracious so while recovering I spent time visiting some of them in China and Australia. Then, upon my return I began to putz around the many lovely anchorages in the area. One day, while out and about I received a radio call from Ritchie saying there was a woman in his office trying to find me. I planned to be back that Sunday evening for dinner at the Russell Boat Club and agreed that I would be willing to meet her there. With her, when I arrived. was a single handed sailor, John Hicks, who had recently entered the bay on his Crealock 34 (designed by the same man and built by the same company as MM Too.) We all chatted about this and that and the evening ended.

The next day, MM Too's engine needed an oil change so I proceeded with what I still think of as a rather nasty job. By now I had what I thought was a rather clever new system that automatically pumped the old oil out to a container. Whoops. Something happened and the hose broke before it reached the container but kept pumping; right at me so before I got it turned off my face and hair and upper body was covered with black used oil. .At that moment I heard a gentle voice call "hello, anybody home?" It was John Hicks. I laughingly invited him aboard if he really wanted to come into this mess. That was our first one on one encounter.

He tells it differently. We were both out walking along the board walk along the beach on the other side of town when we met and I immediately started raving about the Pohutakawas (the New Zealand Christmas Tree) which were in blossom at the moment. He now claims that at that moment he decided I was the woman for him.

Well, I do remember that event also and whatever is the order of events we began to do some buddy boating, something I normally didn't choose to do, and I remember he made a set of flags for each us as a means of communication when we arrived at a destination.: One green, one yellow, and one red. Once the anchors were down we could fly the flags to indicate our preference; red flag for need time to be alone, yellow for whatever, and green for Yeah, let's get together. When we decided to go into Auckland and do some partying he hemmed and hawed before he finally asked, "Do you own a skirt?" Well, sure, but it is down deep somewhere. His solution to that was to go off and buy some fabric and he made a skirt for me.

But John is a person with goals who follows up on his goals and his intent was to circumnavigate so for him it was time to take off for Australia. But the mail flew back and forth and eventually I flew over and joined him in Brisbane and spent a month exploring the Coral Coast. I had made a commitment to friends in Auckland to house sit so this lovely interlude was broken up to get me back to New Zealand. We said goodbye. But, while house sitting, the phone rang. Sailing the wrong direction, i.e. against currents and with unfavorable winds, John had come back to New Zealand. So next we tried a circumnavigation of New Zealand, including Stewart Island on one boat, the Crealock 34.

We then decided this should be a permanent arrangement so it was time to sell MM Too and get it down to one boat which we rechristened Duet. There was no market here for MM Too so John Hicks sailed her single handed non stop to Seattle (7500 miles) while I remained behind continuing to gain strength and caring for Duet.

January of 1998 we married and sailed off together to cross the next two oceans and explore what we saw along the way.

EPILOGUE

I have used the real names of a lot of people and a lot of boats. I hope I haven't made any error in quoting their statements and/or their actions. I used what remains of my logs, journals and memory. I used quite a bit of the latter because so much written data was lost due to the accident between Fiji and New Zealand. All those memories are treasured so they are probably close to accurate but I apologize for any errors.

So many different people helped me so many different times and at so many different places that I am sure I have missed naming some of them. I wish to thank them all whether I named them or not.

Additionally I very much appreciate the encouragement of friends and advisors as I write this and prepare it for publishing.

Last but not least is the encouragement and patience offered by John Hicks, my husband. While I am highly impatient when the software doesn't do what I expect he usually patiently helps solve the problem.We agree that the best thing that happened to us was that fortuitous meeting in New Zealand.

W.S. 1/08

H 7/08

Printed in the United States
95728LV00001B/199/A

9 780979 379703